T0304037

Driving Strategy to Execution Using Lean Six Sigma

A Framework for Creating
High Performance Organizations

Series on Resource Management

Driving Strategy to Execution Using Lean Six Sigma

A Framework for Creating
High Performance Organizations

Gerhard Plenert and Tom Cluley

CRC Press
Taylor & Francis Group
Boca Raton   London   New York

CRC Press is an imprint of the
Taylor & Francis Group, an **informa** business

CRC Press
Taylor & Francis Group
6000 Broken Sound Parkway NW, Suite 300
Boca Raton, FL 33487-2742

© 2012 by Taylor & Francis Group, LLC
CRC Press is an imprint of Taylor & Francis Group, an Informa business

No claim to original U.S. Government works

Version Date: 20120309

International Standard Book Number: 978-1-4398-6713-6 (Hardback)

Visit the Taylor & Francis Web site at
http://www.taylorandfrancis.com

and the CRC Press Web site at
http://www.crcpress.com

Dedication

To the love of my life—
Renee Sangray Plenert
Who makes my life strategic!
And to my kids, their spouses, and of course the grandkids—
Heidi, Dawn, Gregory and Debbie, Gerick, Joshua
and Amy, Natasha and Mark, Zackary, Chelsey,
Lucas, Boston, Evan, Lincoln, and Livy Jay
Who keep my life lean!

Gerhard Plenert

To my loving wife—
Susan Morrison Cluley
Who reminds me that all strategies must be
able to adjust to the realities life presents.
And to my three sons and my daughter-in-law—
Jason, Adam, Erik, and Shelly
Who are on their own paths of executing their strategies.

Tom Cluley

Contents

Preface

Dave, a friend of one of the authors, was telling a story about an interaction he recently had with his son. He had told his son to go clean up his room. His son ran off to his room and, in an attempt to satisfy his father's wishes, proceeded to pick up the first toy he found and put it on the shelf. Dave, walking by the bedroom, told his son; "You haven't picked up your room. Your room is a mess. Get your clothes picked up."*

Again the son, in an attempt to make his father happy, proceeded to pick his clothes up and stuff them in his dresser drawer, regardless of whether they were clean or dirty. But at least they were picked up. Again Dave wasn't satisfied and complained to the son about all the toys that were lying on the floor. Dave's voice was steadily getting louder. He was becoming increasingly agitated, and his son was becoming increasingly frustrated. The son proceeded to pick up the toys and put them on the toy shelf, hoping that he had finally satisfied his father.

But unfortunately Dave was not satisfied and again complained

"Why can't you get your room cleaned up? Look at your schoolbooks that are still lying around, and the papers. Can't you get them cleaned up?" At this point, his son was on the verge of tears, and again, to satisfy his father, he quickly picked up his school materials and put them on his desk.

Finally Dave was satisfied. The room was cleaned up to his satisfaction. But we need to ask, "What was the real problem? Why did it require so many interactions to get the room cleaned? Was the son a disobedient brat? Or should the father have started the process by yelling louder? Does the father need to demonstrate a more aggressive approach?"

Of course the problem is in the communication between Dave and his son. The son didn't understand the strategic goal. Dave had his personal vision of what he expected, and

---

* Story originally told by Dave Sikkelee of Jabil and enhanced by Gerhard Plenert.

the son had his personal interpretation of what was expected, but the two's understanding was not close. Dave was expecting specific results and needed to communicate these results and possibly train his son on how to be successful in achieving the results. Without a strategic perspective, the changes that the son implemented in the room were unsatisfactory. Without strategic direction, it was extremely difficult to achieve the goal. In this case the cost of achieving a goal that was not strategically defined was more than if the father had simply cleaned the room himself.

Of course there is a reason for telling this story. The story is a simplistic version of what happens all the time when change is implemented without a strategic perspective. Companies repeatedly engage in change processes without strategic direction, and the results are similar to what Dave encountered with his son.

Acknowledgments

By Gerhard Plenert

To give credit where credit is due I would need to create a long list of individuals, companies, universities, and countries that I have worked with. In my most recent academic past I have had the pleasure of working with universities like

- University of San Diego in its Supply Chain Management Institute,
- Brigham Young University,
- California State University, Chico, and
- numerous international universities.

Professionally I have had the pleasure of working with organizations such as

- Wipro Consulting as a practice partner in Supply Chain Management
- MainStream Management as a senior strategy and Lean consultant,
- Infosys as a senior principal heading the Lean/Six Sigma/Change Management Practice,
- American Management Systems (AMS) as a senior principal in its Corporate Technology Group, and
- Precision Printers as executive director of Quality, Engineering, Research and Development, Customer Service, Production Scheduling and Planning, and Facilities Management.

Other organizations that I have worked for include

- U.S. Air Force and Department of Defense,
- State of California,
- State of Texas,

- United Nations, and
- many more.

I've lived and worked in factories in Latin America, Asia, and Europe. I have co-authored articles and books and have worked with academics and professionals from as far away as Europe, Japan, and Australia. My broad exposure to a variety of manufacturing and service facilities all over the world has given me the background I needed to write this book.

I need to give special recognition to Tom Cluley, who saved my hide a couple of times when the job market wasn't doing well. MainStream is a great place to work, with an extremely intelligent group of people and a great deal of employee trust. And Tom is extraordinarily supportive to the needs of his employees. I want to especially recognize him and his contribution to this book.

By Tom Cluley

I have had the extreme honor of working with a great number of highly successful and passionate organizations and individuals, and have been fortunate to be in a position to continually learn from my successes and even more so from my failures. I began my Lean journey in earnest as a member of the leadership team within a subsidiary of the Wiremold Company, which at the time was headed by Art Byrne. Art was a passionate practitioner of Lean and provided me with my first understanding that Lean was more than a tool for waste elimination and flow but could be used as a strategic lever for executing an organization's strategy. Art believed in learning from the best. As a result I came in contact with the Lean senseis of Shingijutsu and was lucky enough to gain their counsel over an 8-year period in which, through the use of Lean, we were able to grow the business more than tenfold. During this time we improved virtually every meaningful measure of performance and profitability one could hope to impact, culminating in the sale of the company to the French company Legrand for $505 per share, a dramatic gain from the price of $32 per share when I had joined the company 8 years earlier.

After the sale of the company I became a senior consultant for a major Lean/Six Sigma consulting company. The experience I gained in what worked and what didn't was invaluable. It was in this position that I got the chance to coach, mentor, and facilitate Lean in diverse organizations including manufacturers of appliances, racing wheels, furniture, pool filtering equipment, tires, playground equipment, high-end giftware, and pizza ovens. I also got to facilitate Lean within a film processing company and within the aluminum and lumber industries, where I even had the unique experience of conducting a Lean event with lumberjacks out in the forests of Northern California.

After leaving that position, I had a desire to leverage my knowledge to teach and apply what I had learned. I became a partner in MainStream GS and MainStream Consulting where, for the past 8 years, I have had the honor and pleasure of leading a team of expert consultants helping clients in the private and public sectors create high-performance organizations, leveraging Lean and Six Sigma to execute their strategies. Needless to say, I am surrounded by people, those of my team and my clients, who are much brighter than me and from whom I continue to learn.

I first encountered Gerhard Plenert in 2004, when he became one of our team of senior consultants at MainStream. We had just expanded a Lean pilot converting repair and overhaul of Air Force brake assemblies from batch and queue to cellular flow, into a full-blown continuous process improvement transformation throughout one of the Air Force's Air Logistics Centers. This maintenance, repair, and overhaul (MRO) operation of more than $1 billion provided support to aircraft, missiles, aviation electronics, various commodities, and software support. Additionally the organization had a Material Support Group, as well as a Research Laboratory Group responsible for first article inspection of new parts and components. As a result of the dramatic success we incurred in the pilot, the general in charge strongly encouraged each of his command groups to engage MainStream in supporting improvement efforts within their organizations.

Resistance to change was high at that time, and one of the major resistive groups was the Research Lab. This group comprised top-level engineers and scientists who could not conceive of how some operations people from commercial manufacturing could possibly help them improve the way they conducted business. I met their group director with guns loaded. When he raised the question regarding what qualifications one of my consultants might possibly have that would qualify him to conduct process improvement in his area, I hit him with Gerhard. I informed him that Gerhard was a PhD with more than 20 years of experience who had conducted hundreds of improvement projects throughout the world, not only within industry, but within the public sector, and that he had written and published 7 books (now 10) on various subjects ranging from strategic planning to process improvement. I let him know that Gerhard had been a university professor and an executive director of Quality, Engineering, and Research and Development. Because he was a scientist, I think I had him at PhD.

Gerhard proceeded to run a highly successful project that he highlighted in his book *Reinventing Lean: Introducing Lean Management into the Supply Chain.* Gerhard went his way after that project, but we kept in touch, and about a year and a half ago he rejoined MainStream for about a year to lead a project in which we were called upon to facilitate an Air Force pilot to establish an Air Force–wide strategy alignment and deployment model. Much of his work in this area is highlighted in Part III of this book. It was during this engagement, and after reading a white paper I had written, "Raising the Bar: A Disciplined Approach to Creating High Performance Organizations," that he suggested we co-author this book.

The bulk of the "Model for Success" assessment tool outlined in Part IV's tools for evaluating your strategic capability were developed by my vice president of operations at MainStream GS, Dave Ringel, and his team. Dave is a tireless perfectionist with an unmatched passion for doing what is right for the client and his people.

My final acknowledgment goes to my wife, Susan, who is a constant joy in my life and who provides me a safe haven where I can recharge my batteries and reset my priorities.

Introduction

Too many organizations are failing to be competitive, not because they cannot solve problems, but because they don't know which problems to solve. Resources are being wasted solving nonstrategic problems.

—Gerhard Plenert

The ability to accurately identify barriers to success, define strategies to overcome those barriers, and then focus the limited resources that every organization has on executing those strategies is what differentiates the organization that controls its future from the one that fails.

—Tom Cluley

Anyone can write a book on the procedures behind "strategy" without understanding the key drivers that give a strategy excitement, commitment, and fire. This book is about making a strategy meaningful and powerful. This book will add the critical piece to strategy development, the execution piece, which takes the glossy strategy brochure off the shelf and makes a usable and executable plan. This book will focus on building great strategies and will provide many examples of what makes a strategy great. It will demonstrate how a well-developed strategy generates excitement within an organization. It will offer executives the tools to help them navigate and design a workable and achievable plan for success.

Another element that differentiates this book is that it will go beyond strategy and will add perspective on strategic implementation with tools on making strategy happen, not from a perspective of project management perspective but from a perspective of goal setting, building measures, Balanced Scorecard, and aligning actions. It discusses holding people accountable with team reviews, meetings, and templates for implementation.

This book is unique because it moves beyond the procedural aspects of strategy development and introduces strategic thinking and analysis on a strategic action plan that integrates strategy into execution. Currently, nearly all the strategy books focus on theory, analysis, research, and heavy thinking, which is important and critical. But they do not build a bridge to action. What differentiates this book is that it builds this bridge by demonstrating how to get the right work, the work that will assist in achieving success, accomplished.

The purpose of this book is to provide private companies and government agencies with the tools to

- Understand the power of strategic planning
- Develop a systematic plan for the implementation of strategic principles
- Understand the components of an integrated strategy policy
- Understand the elements that turn a strategy into a plan of action
- Understand the measures that define a world class organization
- Develop a strategy and methodology to introduce strategic principles
- Create a vision and strategy for a world class organization

This book will enhance the reader's interest in developing and sustaining a competitive advantage by developing and sustaining a leading-edge strategy.

The book will discuss how to integrate the strategic tools into an integrated, world class environment. This book will provide professional, objective, and valuable information to solve many of the major strategic management challenges. It will demonstrate solutions to these challenges by using stories and examples of how strategic management improvements have successfully made a difference in both the private and the government sectors.

This book will focus on building great strategies. It will offer a process for creating strategies. This book fills the gap that is being left by many of today's strategy books and will help organizations achieve world class status.

The structure of this book follows the graphic below

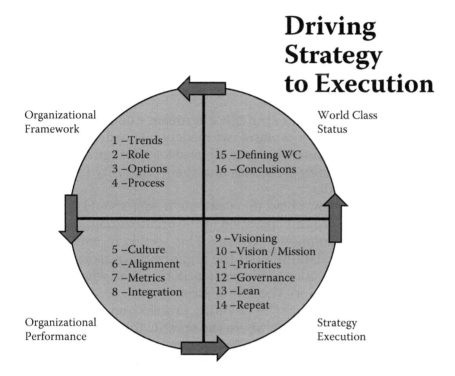

Driving Strategy to Execution

Organizational Framework

World Class Status

1 – Trends
2 – Role
3 – Options
4 – Process

15 – Defining WC
16 – Conclusions

5 – Culture
6 – Alignment
7 – Metrics
8 – Integration

9 – Visioning
10 – Vision / Mission
11 – Priorities
12 – Governance
13 – Lean
14 – Repeat

Organizational Performance

Strategy Execution

Part I: Organizational Framework. This first section discusses the direction of the organization as a whole. Where is a world class, futuristic-looking organization headed? What do we need to get ready for in preparing for the future?

Chapter 1 explores the current and future organizational structure and appropriate trends.

Chapter 2 discusses the role and importance of an organizational strategy. It also explores the role of the strategy in facilitating change.

Chapter 3 explores the various options that exist in developing a strategy and what the various methodologies offer.

Chapter 4 offers some structure for the strategic process that needs to be implemented.

Part II: Organizational Performance Model. This section delves into the details of how a strategic performance model needs to be properly selected and implemented to maximize the overall performance of the organization. This section also discusses the importance of selecting appropriate metrics and integrating them appropriately to achieve the desired organizational goals.

Chapter 5 explores the cultural attributes that are required to create an environment in which strategic plans can be executed and sustained.

Chapter 6 discusses strategic alignment and how it should be deployed. It presents one of two models outlined in this book on a recommended strategic model used for strategy execution.

Chapter 7 analyzes metrics and their criticality in achieving desired results.

Chapter 8 shows how the strategic model should be integrated into the overall operation of the organization.

Part III: Executing the Strategy. This section recommends a methodology for detailing out the organization's strategy and driving it to execution. This section is the *how,* whereas the previous sections were the *why* of strategy.

Chapter 9 describes the visioning process and the scenario planning process. This is where the organization takes a long-range look at its future.

Chapter 10 brings the long-term vision in closer and discusses the development of strategic vision, mission, and customer identification, and then drives these to priorities, end state, and goals. This chapter defines and explains how each of these is used in developing an organizational strategy.

Chapter 11 ties the previous chapters together and focuses on priority-based strategies. It shows how performance metrics should be defined and how tasks are generated.

Chapter 12 brings in the governance of the strategy, explains how performance reviews should work, and explains strategy cascading and communication.

Chapter 13 shows how Lean and Six Sigma should be used to drive the execution of the tasks that were generated by the strategic plan.

Chapter 14 defines how the strategic cycle should be a repetitive, continuous improvement cycle.

Part IV: World Class Strategy Status. This section offers some tools for evaluating your strategic capabilities. Are you world class in your strategy?

Chapter 15 defines what a world class strategic organization would look like. It lists the characteristics and offers an evaluation tool.

Chapter 16 wraps up and summarizes the efforts of this book.

PART I

Organizational Framework

1
Current and Future Organizational Trends

Driving Strategy to Execution

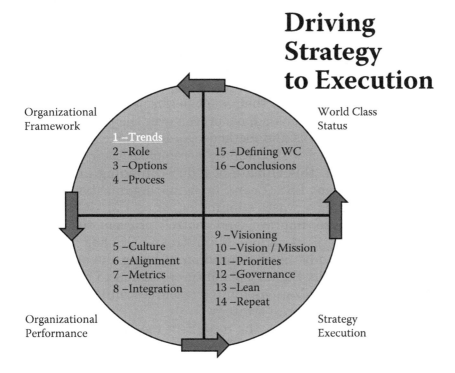

Organizational Framework

World Class Status

1 –Trends	
2 –Role	15 –Defining WC
3 –Options	16 –Conclusions
4 –Process	

5 –Culture	9 –Visioning
6 –Alignment	10 –Vision / Mission
7 –Metrics	11 –Priorities
8 –Integration	12 –Governance
	13 –Lean
	14 –Repeat

Organizational Performance

Strategy Execution

Competition is the keen cutting edge of business, always shaving away at costs.

—Henry Ford

What was true in Henry Ford's day is exponentially true today. The level of competition has risen from local to global, placing enormous stress on both the private and the public sectors alike. The ability to accurately identify barriers to success, define the strategies to overcome those barriers, and then focus the limited resources that every organization has on executing those strategies is what differentiates the organization that controls its future from the one that fails.

MainStream GS, LLC, where one of the authors is a co-owner and where the two authors first met, is a management consulting firm that focuses on creating high-performance organizations through operational excellence. The team of professionals within the company come from successful Lean organizations. They are passionate practitioners who have learned that the organizations that are most likely to succeed under the pressures of a global economy are the ones that execute their strategies by leveraging Lean to create organizational value stream alignment, establish flow, and drive out waste and use Six Sigma to drive out variation in their processes. In addition to their work performed in the private sector, these professionals have proven over the past 10 years that these same tools and methods can help our military and government agencies successfully accomplish their missions and objectives in this climate of reduced funding and manpower. While many LSS (Lean/Six Sigma) organizations focus on Kaizen and pure waste elimination, or on DMAIC (define, measure, analyze, improve, and control) problem solving to eliminate process variation, MainStream GS has evolved their approach to be more focused on utilizing the organization's Lean and Six Sigma capabilities as levers to maximize the use of the organization's limited resources while executing the organization's overall strategy.

From lessons learned, the focus is a top-down/bottom-up approach to implementing CPI (continuous process improvement). CPI, and specifically, methodologies utilizing LSS tools and methods, needs to be a means to an end rather than an end unto itself. This system, which forms a strong foundation for the approach to strategy execution explained in this book, starts with everyone in the client organization having a clear and consistent understanding of the organization's overall mission and their vision for the future. After the mission and vision are clearly defined and articulated, the organization develops a clear understanding of the barriers they face, both now and in the future, that will get in the way of executing their mission and achieving their vision. The organization then develops strategies to overcome those barriers and succeed. These strategies lay the foundation for the projects and events that need to be executed at the various levels of the organization, leveraging their Lean and Six Sigma capabilities. The strategic goals and objectives come from the top down; the execution comes from the bottom up. The essence of this book is to connect the dots, driving strategy to execution to create high-performing organizations.

One of the authors and a few of his associates were at a Logistics Officers Association conference. They had a booth set up to discuss their strategic approach to LSS with various elements of the military logistics community. Several of their competitors were also at the conference. A senior general, who at the time was second in command of a major defense agency, approached the booth and got into a discussion with one of the author's colleagues. The general's agency comprised approximately 26,000 individuals providing worldwide logistics support in both peacetime and wartime to the military services as well as to several civilian agencies and foreign countries. After explaining the company's approach to strategy alignment and deployment, the general said he wanted the author to look at the strategic plan his organization was currently operating under and provide him with an assessment. The general wouldn't say whether he liked his organization's plan or not, but that the author's response would dictate whether or not his company would be invited to the general's headquarters to talk to them further. The general had a copy of his organization's strategic plan forwarded for the assessment. The assessment went as follows:

We thanked the general for allowing us to comment on their strategic plan. The plan appeared well developed and focused. From the details of the plan, we could see that a SWOT (strengths, weaknesses, opportunities, and threats) analysis was performed. We could also see that their planning group took into consideration the external factors likely to impact their mission over the coming years. It was apparent that scenario planning was used to project those likely futures that could impact the direction their strategic plan might need to adjust to. We were able to pick out that the flexibility of the strategies would adjust to the various scenarios that the planners predicted were the most likely to occur. This was definitely one of the better strategic plans we had seen and one not designed to sit on a bookshelf.

The plan discussed three strategic thrusts that appeared well thought out. They had clearly defined statements regarding their mission, vision, values, and goals. The strategy cascaded down into the various elements of the organization and appeared to be focused and achievable. It was encouraging to see that they had decided to use Balanced Scorecard in defining the strategy map for their organization and that they had established key performance metrics by which they would measure success.

Peter Drucker said, "Plans are only good intentions unless they immediately degenerate into hard work." While our assessment determined that they had a very robust set of strategies, we explained that what we have found missing from most strategic plans is the mechanism that takes the strategic plan and translates it from long-term strategies into actionable annual improvement priorities.

We further explained that our preferred methodology for deploying strategy is taken from Hoshin Kanri, which we translate into strategy alignment and deployment (SA&D), a methodology that identifies a critical path to strategy execution and high-level annualized areas of focus. Based on the organization's available resources, the methodology narrows the focus along the critical path to those priorities that can be achieved in a given set of 12-month periods (annual improvement priorities). It then utilizes a three-pronged approach in the deployment process. This approach focuses on the following:

1. Using a consistent technical methodology throughout the organization
2. Creating a governance structure that measures progress, establishes accountability, and provides corrective action
3. Developing a change management plan that creates buy-in and overcomes resistance to change

Michael Hammer in his work on business process reengineering identifies three kinds of processes:

1. Core processes—those that affect the desired delivery of products or services
2. Governing processes—those that create structure and accountability
3. Enabling processes—those that create the environment required to support the core processes

In effect, our three-pronged approach provides the core process of the strategy alignment and deployment; the governance process of providing metrics, oversight and battle rhythm; and the enabling process of the change management plan.

The agency's objectives under each of their strategies seemed to drive the organization in the right direction, but they also appeared to be wide reaching and multiyear focused. Our methodology would help them understand the critical path to execution, breaking those objectives down further into the annual enterprise improvement priorities (AEIPs) with targets and milestones. Then we would cascade those down throughout the organization into actionable levels to build and execute their supporting AIPs (annual improvement priorities) and plans from the bottom up.

We explained that several models come into play in our approach. The first is an understanding of change dynamics. In every organization there are a small number of early adapters, a small number of active resisters, and the rest of the folks as fence sitters waiting to see whether the organization is going to make the shift or not.

It is important to understand that this ratio is independent of function or level of authority in the organization. A few leaders will be early adapters, a few will be active resisters, and the bulk will sit on the fence to see how things are going to go. The same is true of members of the finance team, the operations team, the marketing and sales teams, and the various other elements of the organization. The other important thing to understand is that the active resisters aren't necessarily bad members of the team. In fact, they may be some of the most successful and influential members of the organization.

They just don't want to change, and for good reason. They are successful because they are able to operate effectively in the current environment and feel threatened by change.

During the early period of transition required to execute a long-range strategic plan it is critical to have strong, committed leadership and experienced change agents driving the desired change. Transformation to the desired state is a matter of understanding, acceptance, action, accountability, and learning. The level of support and the kind of support needed throughout an organization's transformation changes as the organization shifts between the various levels of learning and acceptance. Because of this, the change agents must apply situational approaches, based on where the organization is in that transition.

From this basic understanding of the dynamics of change, we apply Dr. John Kotter's 8 Step Process to Leading Change that he defined in his book on the subject, *Leading Change* (Harvard Business Press, 1996). These 8 Steps are as follows:

1. Define the need for change, that is, why we need to adopt the change, what will be the benefit if we do, and what will be the detriment if we don't.
2. Establish a guiding coalition for change, how we are going to organize and engage the key stakeholders of the organization.
3. Establish the vision for what the change will look like, not only as an expression of what leadership desires but of what's in it for the organization as a whole.
4. Communicate the vision throughout the organization; ensure that the entire organization understands the vision.
5. Empower people and remove barriers; create a culture of problem solvers that refuses to work around problems.
6. Secure short-term wins; pick some low-hanging fruit to show that this is going to work, that those that engage are recognized and rewarded.
7. Consolidate gains and keep moving; secure and communicate the gains and encourage others to participate in the success.

8. Anchor the change in new systems and structures; make the new system the current system and enforce the discipline to follow the new standardized work.

This sequence of steps is required to gain momentum and overcome the inherent resistance that every organization has to adopting new systems and methods.

Many organizations are trying to transform through Lean, counting Kaizen events, or through Six Sigma, focusing on the number of black belts they certify. Our approach is to set up the systems and structures for success and to coach leadership on how to create an environment that fosters change acceptance and engagement. We establish the technical implementation skills that personnel need to focus on solving problems and achieving objectives from within their organization. The focus is on creating internal momentum to pass an equilibrium point in which the dynamics of change within the organization overcome the resistance to change and drive the new system from within.

Situational leadership, a model developed by Paul Hersey and Ken Blanchard, sets the approach throughout the process of transformation. In the early stages of transformation, enthusiastic beginners are willing to take on the mantle of change. Unfortunately, they do not have the skills to be successful. As a result, when delegated the task, they often fail to deliver, ultimately losing their enthusiasm and becoming one of the crowd. These enthusiastic beginners, in addition to the formal and informal leaders of the organization, are the ones we seek out and support, the ones we teach, coach, and run interference for. They are the internal change agents of the organization.

Strategy alignment and deployment, ultimately, is about leadership and communication. Along with teaching and coaching the technical elements of SA&D, Lean, Six Sigma, and so forth, working with all levels of leadership is important in coaching and employing change management, organizational development, and leadership tools and methods. We do this on an as-needed basis, using approaches developed by leaders in these fields such as Kotter in *Leading Change*, Jim Collins in *Good to Great*, Blanchard and his aforementioned

Situational Leadership, and many others. Change agents, whether they are internal facilitators or external consultants, need a background in the use of continuous process improvement tools and methods, to be sure; but it is their ability to teach and use the soft skills and tools that enables them to overcome resistance to change.

The major difference in the approach offered in this book is that it does not look at strategy as the purview of leadership and tools such as Lean or Six Sigma as tactical tools for lower levels of the organization. Rather, it looks at strategy as the road an entire organization must take to get to its shared vision and then leverages the tools of Lean and Six Sigma to remove the barriers that get in its way. It is the authors' belief that leadership's responsibility is to

1. Provide its workforce with clear goals and expectations
2. Supply the workforce with the tools, training, and resources to successfully complete their jobs
3. Remove barriers that get in the way of the workforce's success

This is what this book teaches and how it develops and supports strategy execution by establishing a culture of high performance through execution management.

If your organization is successful in executing your strategic plan, then you may not need help right now; but if your organization, like many others, is struggling in its execution, then you need the concepts and methods offered in this book. As Lean/Six Sigma practitioners, the authors realize how critical it is to look at products and services in terms of value streams, and as such we know how critical the supply chain is to the value stream. Your organization or agency more than likely provides a critical link in the chain of everything that occurs in the support of your customers. Helping you to align your organization to the current and future needs of your customers and to address and overcome your barriers to achieving your strategic goals and objectives is the reason why the authors are writing this book.

Concluding the story regarding the general and his agency, the author's team received an invitation and six weeks later was at the agency's headquarters speaking with their top strategy people. The author and client discussed the client's concerns that their strategy had indeed stalled and further discussed the author's perspective on why the organization was not making any gains.

There are several reasons why strategic plans do not get executed, but the main reason is that, for most organizations, strategic planning is something that organizations do separately from their day-to-day operations—if they do it at all. When completed, the strategic plan provides overarching guidance, but very few organizations link it directly to the way they operate or build it into their daily activities. They do not create the cascading alignment nor the governance structures required to ensure disciplined execution. They also fail to understand and address the resistance to change inherent in every organization and how that resistance to change thwarts leadership in their desire to execute their strategies.

If this is how it has always been, why change? After all, this cascading of plans, setting up of governance systems, measuring performance, and overcoming resistance to change seems like a lot of work. Organizations are already stressed and overworked. They don't have time for this, and besides, they seem to be able to survive without it.

The fact of the matter is that what got us to where we are today just won't get us to where we need to be in the future. The strain on resources and the pressure to get more out of those resources is just too much for an organization to bear unless they change the fundamental way they plan and execute. This is true whether an organization is a commercial endeavor competing for business in a global economy, or a public entity that is trying to get the most mission capability out of limited funding and limited resources. Simply reacting to the changing pressures that face most organizations will eventually lead them to the breaking point. Understanding barriers, current ones and those likely to hit in the future, developing viable strategies to overcome those barriers, and then executing those strategies via a robust methodology for aligning available resources enable an organization to focus its resources in such a way as to overcome those barriers and succeed. In the commercial world it's an easy equation. The organization that does the best wins. In the public sector, especially that of the military, failure is not an option.

In the future, pressure to be more effective and more efficient will only increase. Throwing more resources at problems is no longer an option. As the authors are writing this book, heated arguments are going on between members of Congress regarding the federal budget. The outlook for future budgets doesn't look to be any easier. The conservatives want to roll back government spending, shrink government, and lower the deficit. The liberals want to improve infrastructure, education, and health care, yet maintain a robust defense, Social Security, and Medicare, while also shrinking the deficit. The federal debt is going through the roof with ever-increased borrowing from China and other creditors that are not necessarily our friends. The reality of the situation is that if the right and the left could come together in developing a common vision for the future and execute a strategic plan to eliminate waste in government programs, then everyone could have what they want and the American taxpayers would receive dramatically improved services with much more money in their pockets. At the same time, businesses would be able to receive the benefit of reductions in corporate taxes, which are currently some of the highest in the industrial world. Everyone recognizes this, but to date our leaders lack the common vision or the ability to agree on an effective strategy. They also appear to lack the political will or know-how to execute. As a result, the resource gap is growing and the strain on the system is beginning to impact our ability to sustain the current state.

Similar financial and competitive pressures are placing demands on industry and business. The organization that understands the barriers it will face and is able to establish and drive effective strategies to overcome those barriers is that one that will flourish. Organizations that don't will most likely fail.

As we think about what strategies we need to execute, we need to be sure that those strategies are focused—not only on the current barriers we face today but on those we anticipate will occur in the future. The more accurate and complete our strategic roadmaps are, and the more effective we are at executing our strategies, the better chance we will have of achieving our vision. Most organizations take three to four iterations of SA&D before they become marginally successful in aligning their organizations in a manner that drives dramatic annual improvement. In this book we will share our experiences so that the reader has the opportunity to shorten that cycle. The best time to start is now.

2

The Role of Strategy in Organizing Change

Driving Strategy to Execution

Organizational Framework

- 1 –Trends
- 2 –Role
- 3 –Options
- 4 –Process

World Class Status

- 15 –Defining WC
- 16 –Conclusions

Organizational Performance

- 5 –Culture
- 6 –Alignment
- 7 –Metrics
- 8 –Integration

- 9 –Visioning
- 10 –Vision / Mission
- 11 –Priorities
- 12 –Governance
- 13 –Lean
- 14 –Repeat

Strategy Execution

If you don't know where you are going, any road will get you there.

—Lewis Carroll

Most organizations change as a reaction to the various impacts on day-to-day operations. While this method of adaptation tends to respond to the need for change, it does so in a tactical manner, often at a cost to efficiency, suboptimizing the organization as a whole. *Strategy* looks at both the current conditions and the potential future conditions in an effort to define the changes the organization must make to meet the future needs of either the customer or the mission while achieving the desired long-range goals and objectives of the organization. Having an effective strategy enables the organization to *pro*actively affect change in an efficient and effective manner, rather than *re*actively in a manner that not only wastes resources but may inadvertently drive the organization down a road to failure.

Prior to consulting, one of the authors was a senior leader within a subsidiary organization of the Wiremold Company. Wiremold was a 100-year-old family-owned business that manufactured Wire Management Products. Wiremold had recently hired Art Byrne as chief executive officer to run their operations, which included three subsidiary companies, one of which the author joined shortly after Art took charge. Wiremold's success in Lean is well documented in James Womack's and Daniel Jones's *Lean Thinking*, as well as in Bob Emiliani's book *Better Thinking, Better Results*.

As one of the individuals helping to drive the organization's success, the author realized only in hindsight that the continuous efforts to identify and eliminate waste were not the primary driver of Wiremold's success as a company. It was the fact that they used Lean to execute a larger strategy of growing their base of operations through strategic acquisitions, expanding both their products and their markets. They leveraged their Lean expertise to free up cash that funded those acquisitions. They had a growth and profitability strategy and executed it by leveraging Lean, not the other way around.

Many organizations during the past decade or so have tried to leverage Lean, Six Sigma, and other continuous improvement methodologies to drive their success, only to find that while they accomplished waste reduction and made nice gains in the way they operated, they failed to sustain those gains and they also failed to move the big bars that measure success and failure at a corporate level. As a result, their efforts tended to stall or die outright. This is because they took a tactical approach to continuous process improvement rather than a strategic one and because they changed processes but failed to change people. Sun Tzu stated, "Strategy without tactics is the slowest route to victory. Tactics without strategy is the noise before defeat." Implementing Lean without having a strategic plan to leverage gains often becomes the noise before defeat as improvements slip and people lose faith in the process. Failing to surround improved processes with governance or to engage the workplace in supporting the desired change leads to slippage and the inability to sustain those improvements.

It is surprising how many organizations fail to develop a strategy that is well communicated to and understood by its workforce. It is also surprising how many organizations fail to see strategy as a means to a long-range end.

Several years ago a friend of one of the authors, who owns and runs a successful machine shop, asked about the work the author's consulting company performed. He knew that the company had a foundation in Lean and Six Sigma, and he was interested in applying those principles in his company. As discussions progressed the friend let the author know that he had a concern. The author's friend was in his mid-60s and he had no plan regarding how to transition his company as he grew older. He had about 40 people working for him and was worried that without a transition plan, if something were to happen to him, the company would fold.

The discussion led to strategic planning and strategy deployment, and the question was raised, "What do you want things to look like in 5 years?" The friend asked what the author meant, so the author probed further, asking if his friend wanted to sell the company or shut it down, or if he wanted to turn the company over to his workforce, or even if he saw himself still working but having more of the operation being run by his internal management. The author explained that depending on the desired outcome, he would want to execute a different set of strategies. If he wanted to sell, he might be hesitant to buy any additional capital equipment and might want to take steps to maximize his income statement and improve those ratios that a buyer would be interested in. If he wanted to shut it down, he might want to have a plan to begin selling off pieces of the business and equipment. If he wanted to turn the company over to the workforce, he would need to pass on his skills to members of the organization, as he had created a situation in which he was at the center of things and had his hands in all of the key elements of the operation. If he wanted to keep his hand in but turn over more of the operations to his internal management, he might want to improve cash flow so that he could pay internal managers for their increased responsibilities and still keep his profits at a level that would pay him his desired rate even though he was actively reducing his participation in the company.

The author's friend had not seriously looked beyond the demands of the immediate quarter and as such had to think about what he wanted for the future. As he thought about what the company meant to him and how much he enjoyed working, he decided that the last option was the right one for him. He began an aggressive Lean program in his company to drive out waste and improve cash flow. He also identified a few key individuals and began to train them on how to design computer-aided drafting programs, quote to customers, and oversee operations on the production floor—activities that he had held close over the years. He identified some new product lines and bought some low-priced machines that were on the market due to some competitors shutting down.

Now 5 years later, he continues to run his company but takes extended trips with his wife, driving around the country in his motor home, while others in the company fill in during his absence. He couldn't be happier. He knows that if something were to happen to him, the company would continue to run, supplying his wife, who does the company's bookkeeping and accounting, with income and providing jobs for the workforce. It turns out that 5 years earlier the workforce had the same concerns for the future of the company, and many of them were looking to possibly jump ship. After the author's friend began training others in the company how to do the things he once held close, the concerns of the workforce vanished. As he executed his Lean conversion, they became energized and felt good about themselves and their future.

Strategy creates a vision for the entire organization. Successfully executing that strategy creates cohesion and allows an organization to change in a manner that achieves its objectives.

When thinking about organizations in terms of what changes they need to execute to satisfy their customers and execute their mission, it helps to understand that organizations are systems made up of various processes. They have *core processes* that directly add value for the customer. Their *enabling processes* are those that help support the organization and develop the environment from which they can conduct core processes. And they have *governing processes* that provide rules and structure to the organization, along with maintaining accountability and providing corrective action.

This author had the pleasure of watching Michael Hammer present these concepts, which are at the heart of business process reengineering, to a group of senior leaders of the Air Force Air Mobility Command. Hammer's presentation was entertaining in addition to being informative. In it he laid out the problem of how traditional organizations are established in functional stovepipes, and how inefficient it is to conduct functional processes in isolation and then catapult them to the next functional stovepipe, or "castle" as he described it. To the author, as a Lean practitioner, this reinforced the concepts of value stream management, flow, and waste elimination.

The functional orientation obtained when pursuing careers tends to formulate stovepipe thinking. This is due not only to the heavy focus on a specific discipline but also on the social structures formed around professional associations. As a result, challenges to eliminate waste and improve are looked at through functional lenses. This then results in a process that makes the functional organization work better but often at the expense of the value stream, which in turn also, as noted above with reactive versus proactive change, suboptimizes the organization as a whole. This is the same dynamic at work when individual departments or divisions look at corporate strategic plans without the systems and structures defined in this book. They look at them through their own paradigms and develop their plans accordingly. The result is a lack of true alignment and a large number of poorly executed long-range projects, most of which fail to be completed before the next round of strategic planning. The overall organization fails to achieve the kinds of significant gains required to remain competitive or achieve its goals and objectives.

Summary

As pricing and cost pressures mount, organizations will be forced to focus on dramatically reducing the cost of doing business. They will need to improve their value streams, removing as much waste as possible to reduce overall cost to the customer, and improve their response time to meeting the customer's needs, while maintaining 100 percent quality.

To do so, not only will they need to have strategies that affect change to their core process, but they will most likely need to change their governing and enabling process as well. Effective strategies will enable them to take a systems approach to changing the organization and organizing the change.

3

Strategic Models
A Plethora of Options

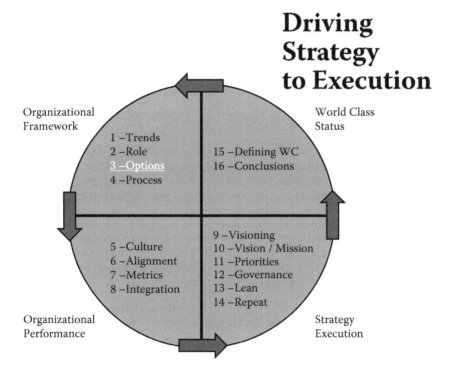

Driving Strategy to Execution

Organizational Framework

1 –Trends
2 –Role
3 –Options
4 –Process

World Class Status

15 –Defining WC
16 –Conclusions

5 –Culture
6 –Alignment
7 –Metrics
8 –Integration

9 –Visioning
10 –Vision / Mission
11 –Priorities
12 –Governance
13 –Lean
14 –Repeat

Organizational Performance

Strategy Execution

While preparing for this chapter I decided to Google *strategic planning methodologies* and came up with 1,460,000 results. Strategic planning has been around since armies first planned wars. Wikipedia provides the etymology of *strategic* as coined in English in 1825 of military origin, from the Greek (*strategikos*), "of or for a general," from (*strategos*), "leader or commander of an army, general," a compound of (*stratos*), "army, host" +, "leader, chief," in turn from (*ago*), "to lead." The *strategoi*, as a council of advisors, provided the ruler with advice on how to win wars as opposed to winning tactical battles. Business leaders today still make references to the strategies explained in *The Art of War*, written in the sixth century B.C. by Sun Tzu.

There are various methods and approaches to strategic planning, and all attempt to answer at least one of the three following areas:

1. Defining the organization's purpose
2. Defining the organization's customers and what their expectations and needs are
3. Defining the current state of the organization against a desired future state and answering the question of how the organization gets from here to there

Strategic planning, at its heart, lays the foundation for strategic management.

> Strategic management is an ongoing process that evaluates and controls the business and the industries in which the company is involved; assesses its competitors and sets goals and strategies to meet all existing and potential competitors; and then reassesses each strategy annually or quarterly (i.e., regularly) to determine how it has been implemented and whether it has succeeded or needs replacement by a new strategy to meet changed circumstances, new technology, new competitors, a new economic environment, or a new social, financial, or political environment.
>
> **—Robert Boyden Lamb**
> Competitive Strategic Management *(Prentice Hall, 1984, p. ix)*

The first strategic planning process for U.S. business was developed at the Harvard Business School in the 1920s. According to Phillip Blackberry, MPAff, in an article he wrote entitled, "History of Strategic Planning" (originally published in *Armed Forces Comptroller*, vol. 39, no. 1, Winter 1994, pp. 23–24), this model defines *strategy* as a pattern of purposes and policies defining the company and its business. He further states that "a strategy is a common thread or underlying logic that holds a business together. The firm weaves purpose and policies in a pattern that unites company resources, senior management, market information, and social obligations. Strategies determine organizational structure; appropriate strategies lead to improved economic performance."

In the 1950s the focus of strategic planning began to shift away from the holistic approach of defining the firm to one of managing risk. As companies began to merge into conglomerates, this became what the business community termed the *portfolio model* of strategic planning. The portfolio model made the assumption that by diversifying a portfolio of companies, products, and services, a corporation would mitigate the risk associated with having "all of it eggs in one basket." The weakness of this approach is that it fails to create a lever for continuous improvement and strategic focus within a particular element of the corporate conglomerate.

In the 1960s through the 1970s, strategic planning evolved and refocused on becoming a lever for creating a competitive advantage, focusing on productivity and profits. The strategic planning process, while varied in method, focuses on three basic steps:

1. Define the current condition through some form of environmental scan.
2. Establish goals and objectives for the future.
3. Develop a roadmap or plan for execution.

The most commonly used methodology to define the current condition is the SWOT analysis, the process of identifying the organization's strengths, weaknesses, opportunities, and threats, which is accredited to Albert Humphrey, who led a convention at Stanford University studying data from Fortune 500 companies. This is often further amplified by developing a common understanding of external factors that might impact the organization. One form of this is a PETERS analysis, which lists the political, environmental, technical, economic, regulatory, and sociological impact factors.

Setting goals and objectives involves a more objective approach dictated by the outcomes desired of the leadership.

Many organizations attempt to develop SMART objectives (specific, measurable, achievable, realistic, and time sensitive).

The manner in which the various methodologies develop their roadmap offers the most diversity in methodologies. The Balanced Scorecard, developed by Robert S. Kaplan and David P. Norton, identifies four perspectives through which an organization should develop its strategy:

1. *Financial.* To succeed financially, how should we appear to our shareholders?
2. *Internal business process.* To satisfy our stakeholders and customers, what business process must we excel at?
3. *Customer.* To achieve our vision, how should we appear to our customers?
4. *Learning and growth.* To achieve our vision, how will we sustain our ability to change and improve?

Each of these in turn requires the development of objectives, measures, targets, and initiatives.

Another methodology for developing a strategic plan or roadmap involves scenario planning. Scenario planning is an adaptation of the traditional military planning methodology that was further developed after World War II by Herman Kahn of the Rand Corporation at the Hudson Institute (Kees Van Der Heijen, *Scenarios: The Art of Strategic Conversation*, Wiley, 2003). It was further developed for business by Pierre Wack at Royal Dutch Shell. The basic process of scenario planning follows six steps:

1. Identify drivers for change and assumptions, including predetermines.
2. Draw drivers into a viable framework.
3. Produce a number of potential future scenarios.
4. Reduce these to a few of the most likely futures.
5. Draw up the likely future scenarios and identify early indicators.
6. Develop strategies that are able to adjust to the likely futures and adjust as early indicators trigger that a scenario is about to unfold.

Assumption-based planning (ABP) is another strategic planning methodology. It was developed by Morlie Hammer Levin and James A. Dewar of the Rand Corporation in 1987 (James Dewar, *Assumption-Based Planning: A Tool for Reducing Avoidable Surprises*, Cambridge University Press, 2002). The five steps in ABP are as follows:

1. Identify the assumptions in the plan.
2. Identify the assumptions upon which the plan most heavily rests ("load bearing").
3. Develop signposts—warning signs that a surprise is about to occur.
4. Develop shaping actions used to shore up uncertain assumptions.
5. Develop hedging actions—prepare for the possibility that an assumption will fail.

By the 1980s strategic planning began to wane. Ineffective execution, despite companies putting large efforts into the strategic planning process, raised questions regarding return on investment. With the success and subsequent focus on the Toyota Production System, Hoshin Planning began to generate new interest in strategic planning.

> The importance of implementing this concept [Hoshin Kanri] began sometime before 1645 when Miyamoto Musashi wrote *A Book of Five Rings* as a guide to samurai warriors. The basis of this philosophy was summed up in one word: heiho, or strategy. The word *hieho* is formed from two Chinese characters: *hei* meaning soldier, and *ho* meaning method or form... Hoshin is related to heiho in kendo, Mushashi's martial art of sword fighting with katana. The word Hoshin is composed of two Chinese characters ho and shin; ho meaning method or form and shin meaning shiny needle or compass. Taken together the word "hoshin" means a "methodology for strategic direction setting."
>
> **—Greg Watson**
> *Director of corporate quality, Compaq Computer Corp.,*
> *Introduction in* Hoshin Kanri Policy Deployment for Successful
> TQM, *by Yoji Akao (Productivity Press, English translation 1991)*

As a senior member of one of the Wiremold Companies, one of the authors was introduced to Hoshin Kanri by master

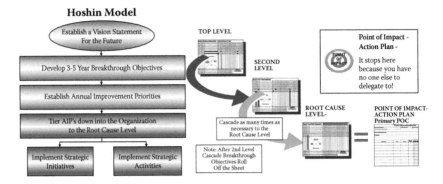

Figure 3.1 Hoshin model.

senseis of Shingijutsu. The basic structure of Hoshin Kanri is as follows (see Figure 3.1):

1. Develop the organization's vision.
2. Develop the organization's mission statement.
3. Conduct an analysis of the current environment.
4. Develop the breakthrough objectives (BTOs) required to achieve the vision.
5. Develop annual improvement priorities (AIPs).
6. Assign primary responsibility and secondary responsibility for each of the AIPs.
7. Establish AIP metrics and targets.
8. Cascade AIPs down through each level of the organization until you reach the actionable level of the organization, conducting catchball at each level.
9. Develop an X-matrix defining activities, targets, and responsible individuals for each level of the Hoshin plan.
10. Develop planning sheets for each of the actionable plans.
11. Develop "bowling charts" to track month-by-month progress.
12. Conduct periodic reviews.
13. Repeat.

While this methodology worked very well at Wiremold, attempting to implement this methodology in organizations that did not have the culture of change acceptance or the discipline of a robust governance system that existed in Wiremold resulted in poorly sustained efforts. Root cause analysis of the problem indicated that the technical elements of their plans were sound. It was the cultural acceptance and lack of a robust and disciplined governance system that were lacking, revealing the need for a more balanced approach.

Summary

The key to successfully using strategic planning is to take it out of the purview of the stovepiped planning functions where much of strategic planning resides and make it a living document that drives executable action plans throughout the organization, making it part of the daily activity. This requires an integration of an executable methodology, combined with robust governance, as well as a managed plan to overcome the inherent resistance to change that always exists in all organizations. This book will show the reader how that is done.

4
The Strategic Process

Driving Strategy to Execution

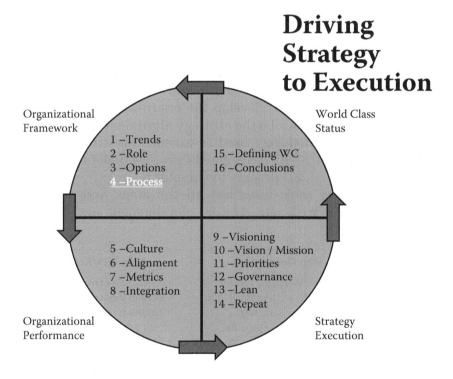

Organizational Framework

Organizational Performance

World Class Status

Strategy Execution

1 –Trends
2 –Role
3 –Options
4 –Process

5 –Culture
6 –Alignment
7 –Metrics
8 –Integration

15 –Defining WC
16 –Conclusions

9 –Visioning
10 –Vision / Mission
11 –Priorities
12 –Governance
13 –Lean
14 –Repeat

If you are planning for one year, grow rice. If you are planning for 20 years, grow trees. If you are planning for centuries, grow men.

—Chinese proverb

The strategic process depends on how far out into the future the organization is looking. The focus of various levels along with typical planning horizons follows:

Operating unit	Near-term strategic planning	Up to 1 year
Operating division	Short-term strategic planning	1 to 6 years
Company	Mid-term strategic planning	6 to 10 years
Corporation	Long-term planning	10 to 30 years
Industry	Far-range planning	30+ years

We will discuss mid- to long-range planning in more detail through our discussions on visioning and scenario planning in Chapter 9. Currently we will focus on the more operational view of strategy development, typically looking out 3 to 5 years.

The strategic process that links strategy to execution begins with the development of the overarching strategy. Steps 1 through 4 in the table that follows define our approach to the process we use to develop the organization's strategy. Steps 5 through 9 describe the strategy alignment and deployment (SA&D) methodology used to execute the strategy. We will discuss the strategy development process in detail in this chapter and the SA&D process in Chapter 6.

The following table describes all the steps and deliverables associated with our strategy development and SA&D methodology.

Step #	Step Description	Activities/Results
1 Research Findings and Analysis	Form the enterprise executive council into a Steering Team to provide consistency, integration, and systems learning. Steering Team composed of senior leader, senior staff, and selected members. Get support from every member of the steering team for the overall strategy and SA&D effort. Establish ground rules.	• Initial meeting with senior leader. • Develop interview sheets and surveys if desired. • Conduct interviews/ surveys. • Summarize findings and establish common themes. Report on interview and survey findings and review with senior leader.

Step #	Step Description	Activities/Results
	Identify the organization's mission and vision, if they exist, or gather relevant data regarding what key staff members believe the mission and vision are. Collect initial data utilizing surveys and/or interviews to determine barriers. Work with key client personnel to establish suppliers, inputs, processes, outputs, and customers (SIPOCs), and enterprise value stream maps if appropriate. Use these discussions to probe into barriers and identify areas of concern and opportunity.	• Finalize initial report and forward to Steering Team/executive council as a read-ahead. • Establish strategic Steering Team or executive council and set first session.

The next table describes all the steps and deliverables associated with our strategy development and SA&D methodology.

Step #	Step Description	Activities/Results
2 First Session	Develop or confirm the mission and the enduring vision for the organization as a basis to generate enthusiasm and direction for an organization-wide SA&D plan. Identify critical success factors for the organization. Develop consensus among Steering Team members regarding the current reality of the organization. Review and validate findings. Review survey results. Understand and agree on the need for change and where change needs to occur (people, resources, process and performance).	• Common understanding of present situation. • Mission and vision developed/confirmed. • Strategic 3–5 year breakthrough objectives (BTOs) established. • Develop 3–5 year annual focus areas based on critical path and leader's intent. • Provide summary report on methodology used, results, findings, and recommendations.

Continued

Step #	Step Description	Activities/Results
	Identify key elements that must fundamentally change within the organization in order to overcome Barriers and Achieve the Vision. Develop 3–5 year Breakthrough Objectives (BTOs) around these key elements.	
	Identify high level 3-5 year annualized focus areas and critical path to executing the overall SA&D.	
3 Second Session	Establish the criteria for robust enterprise-level annual improvement priorities. They must have targets that are measurable, quantifiable, and qualitative. They must have a scheduled delivery and we must define the resources we are going to allocate to them.	• Common understanding of present situation. • Mission and vision developed/confirmed. • Strategic 3–5 year BTOs established. • Develop 3–5 year annual focus areas based on critical path and commander's intent.
	Establish annual enterprise improvement priorities (AEIPs). AEIPs are goals that can be achieved within the next 12 months that will support the 3–5 year breakthrough objectives (BTOs) and the 3–5 year plan. From the AEIPs, projects and activities will be identified to yield immediate and annual results.	• Provide summary report on methodology used, results, findings and recommendations. • Alignment among continuous process improvement (CPI) Steering Team, mission support, and the various local leaders.
	Form and charter a subteam to identify and pitch AEIP key performance metrics to the Steering Team.	• Establish AEIPs. • Launch catchball. • Conduct catchball (between sessions).
	Define and establish the need for catchball. Catchball is an important part of the SA&D process; it involves active dialogue between the top leadership of the organization and the remaining tiers below it. The purpose of this process is to	• Report on methodology used, results, findings and recommendations. • Postsession, upon completion of catchball, report on finalized AIPs in support of AEIPs to team.

Step #	Step Description	Activities/Results
	assess current initiatives, clarify and refine the BTOs, and then validate the AEIPs—this is one of the most powerful, yet underutilized, processes to achieve consensus and readiness for mission execution. Between the second and third sessions the senior staff will conduct catchball with their staff members, establish their supporting AIPs, and set target levels for improvement within their part of the organization. They will also negotiate these with the senior leader.	
4 Third Session	Each member presents their AIPs in support of AEIPs. Finalize AEIPs based on AIP commitments and agree on metrics from Step 3. The strategy map is developed. a. Review Kotter's 8 Step Process to Leading Change and develop change management plan. b. Develop scoring methodology (such as Balance Scorecard) to track and report progress. Establish governance structure complete with review schedules and leader's standard work. c. Identify the steps to be taken going forward that will flesh out the AIPs.	• Personnel knowledge of the CPI plan and how it fits in the daily lives. • Strategy map, Balanced Scorecard, and governance structure. • Customized CPI implementation plan for the organization. • List of activities and performance metrics that will support the AEIPs. • Provide final report draft and final report.

Continued

Step #	Step Description	Activities/Results
5	The organization now begins to develop their execution plans and implement its CPI projects and rapid improvement events to support and fulfill the AEIPs. The number of projects occurring at the same time will depend upon the capacity of the business units and the Steering Team to lead and manage the changes identified in Step 4. However, the goal will be to begin with a few projects, show quick success, and ramp up to many projects across the organization, fueling the ramp up through resources freed up as a result of improvement projects.	• CPI projects begin. • Improved organization processes. • Infectious enthusiasm for CPI begins to develop, leading to cultural change.
6	The weekly, monthly, and quarterly reviews ensure that the activities and results of the CPI projects and events toward the AEIPs are tracked via the metrics previously agreed upon.	• Report of CPI activities, implementations, results, and plans from both a technical and cultural standpoint. • Corrective action plan in place when required for CPI events and cultural change. • Plans and actions refined and redeployed.
7	When planned activities fall behind schedule or do not meet expected results, there must be an analysis of the root cause and corrective action taken to either get back on track or make adjustments in the plan itself. The corrective action process accomplishes this via problem-solving techniques with a Plan-Do-Check-Act thought process.	• Annual review with lessons learned. • Improved SA&D for next year. • Culture within the organization begins to shift toward CPI.

Step #	Step Description	Activities/Results
8	At the end of the first year, the plan will be reviewed to determine if the projects contributed to the AEIPs. In addition, for review will be the entire strategic CPI plan, including lessons learned from each project.	
9	Preparation for next year's plan are made addressing corrective actions and new requirements (repeat Steps 3 through 9).	• Next year's SA&D plan. • Rolling 5-year plan.

Vision versus Mission

Experts differ on whether the vision or the mission sets the tone for developing strategies. In fact, many organizations use the terms *vision* and *mission* interchangeably. To move forward we offer these simple definitions: *Mission* defines an organization's purpose. *Vision* defines the future state an organization wishes to attain. In both cases the reason for defining these things is to create a common understanding of who we are and where we are trying to go. Without this common understanding, elements of the organization set out on their own path, applying valuable resources toward achieving objectives that may in fact suboptimize the organization's ability to successfully execute its mission or achieve its vision. Strategies are those things that align the application of our resources to ensure that we can successfully conduct our mission and achieve our vision for the future. Because of this the authors believe that the strategic process begins with an understanding and agreement regarding the overall mission or purpose of the organization. Jim Collins, in *Good to Great*, while not specifically calling it a mission, establishes excellent criteria for defining an organization's purpose with his Hedgehog Principle. He tells a story about the hedgehog and the fox in which the fox is cunning and tries many different ways to attack the hedgehog, but the hedgehog does one thing exceedingly well, which is to roll up into a ball when under attack, using its spines to ward off the attacker. Then he states that great organizations have a hedgehog focus on what they do. Their hedgehog defines the thing they have a passion to do, the thing they believe they can be the best at in the world, and the thing that drives their economic engine.

Some examples of mission statements include the following:

Aetna is dedicated to helping people achieve health and financial security by providing easy access to safe, cost-effective, high-quality health care and protecting their finances against health-related risks.

—Aetna mission statement

Our mission declares our purpose as a company. It serves as the standard against which we weigh our actions and decisions. It is the foundation of our Manifesto.

To refresh the world in body, mind and spirit.
To inspire moments of optimism through our brands and our actions.
To create value and make a difference everywhere we engage.

—Coca-Cola mission statement

To make people happy.

—Walt Disney Company mission statement

To discover, develop and deliver innovative medicines that help patients prevail over serious diseases.

—Bristol-Myers Squibb Company mission statement

We are a global family with a proud heritage, passionately committed to providing personal mobility for people around the world.

—Ford Motor Company mission statement

Our mission is to operate the best specialty retail business in America, regardless of the product we sell. Because the product we sell is books, our aspirations must be consistent with the promise and the ideals of the volumes which line our shelves. To say that our mission exists independent of the product we sell is to demean the importance and the distinction of being booksellers. As booksellers we are determined to be the very best in our business, regardless of the size, pedigree or inclinations of our competitors. We will continue to bring our industry nuances of style and approaches to bookselling which are consistent with our evolving aspirations. Above all, we expect to be a credit to the communities we serve, a valuable resource to our customers, and a place where our dedicated booksellers can grow and prosper. Toward this end we will not only listen to our customers and booksellers but embrace the idea that the Company is at their service.

—Barnes & Noble mission statement

The last two, Ford and Barnes & Noble, identify an important element of an organization's mission. Both of these companies have had recent struggles. Ford's mission statement, "We are a global family with a proud heritage, passionately committed to providing personal mobility for people around the world," avoids the specific product "providing personal mobility for people" and allows for the organization to adjust to changes in technology. Barnes & Noble, within the content of its mission statement, states, "Because the product *we sell is books* [emphasis added], our aspirations must be consistent with the promise and the ideals of the *volumes which line our shelves* [emphasis added]. To say that our mission exists independent of the product we sell is to demean the importance and the distinction of being booksellers." This statement, while staying true to the elements in Collins's Hedgehog Principle, appears to narrow their focus in a manner that may potentially make them the modern-day buggy whip manufacturer, should they fail to adjust to the technological innovations that are rapidly making hardcover books on shelves less and less in demand. Faced with an unfolding scenario of more and more people turning to downloadable devices with instant access, they have launched the Nook. It will be interesting to see whether they revise their mission statement in a manner that focuses on supplying the content of books rather than the paper products that currently line their shelves.

Establishing an organization's vision is a trickier matter. As noted in Chapter 2, an organization's vision is dependent on where it wants or needs to be in the future. That in turn can be dependent on the desires of leadership or the imperatives of the environment that the future might present. Many different things drive an organization or a leader of an organization. While the majority of private sector organizations are driven by profit, there are exceptions. Some are driven to maintain a certain quality of life or a passion to purpose as noted in the Hedgehog Principle. Many public sector and nonprofit organizations are driven by their mission. In either case, current and future barriers may be the impetus behind a stated vision. An example of the latter became obvious when one of the authors was consulting for the U.S. Air Force Air Mobility Command. His company was chosen to help them begin their Lean journey executing what the Air Force called AFSO21 (Air Force Smart Operations for the 21st Century). The Air Mobility Command is one of the 10 Major Commands (MAJCOMs) of the U.S. Air Force. It is responsible for providing global outreach for the country's military, transporting goods and personnel, including the president of the United States in Air Force One, VIPs, and Joint Forces personnel in support of the war efforts and disaster relief around the world. It is also responsible for mid-air refueling of aircraft.

The team began their strategy session in a facilitated meeting with the four-star commander; his immediate staff of generals and command colonels; and the commander of the 18th Air Force, the execution arm of the command supporting TRANSCOM (Transportation Command), the joint deployment and distribution enterprise responsible for global support of joint, U.S. government, and Secretary of Defense–approved multinational and nongovernmental logistical requirements. Defining the Air Mobility Command's mission was fairly simple; after some exercises and discussions of various iterations, they came up with, "Provide Global Air Mobility... Right Effects, Right Place, Right Time." Defining Air Mobility Command's vision for the future proved to be more challenging. They rightfully claimed that their vision was to be the best in the world but argued that they already were, so why have a vision that was separate from their mission. We began to discuss the current state of things impacting the command.

Their current reality was a "perfect storm" regarding the need for change. With two war efforts going on at the time, and numerous requirements to support disaster relief in response to things like the Thai tsunami and Hurricane Katrina, the demands for their service were at an all-time high, with no likelihood of diminishing. Due to federal funding constraints and problems in their acquisition process, they had been unable to fund new replacement aircraft to support their mission. Their aircraft were getting older. The KC-135 refueling aircraft had just had its 50th birthday, and as they liked to state, with the current schedule for replacing it, the mother of the last KC-135 pilot had yet to be born. To add to their resource problems they had also just undergone PBD 720 (Program Budget Decision 720), a congressionally mandated reduction in manning, and were looking at a future with additional funding cuts. In other words, with demand for services high and growing, aging aircraft that required ever-increasing repair and maintenance, less personnel, and less money to work with, their ability to maintain their current level of mission capability might be in jeopardy if they continued to operate as normal. To maintain their superiority it was imperative that they become more efficient as well as more effective in executing their mission. After much debate and in response to the barriers they were facing, their vision became, "Unrivaled Global Reach for America... Always!" the key being the "...Always!"

Strengths, Weaknesses, Opportunities, and Threats

The above discussion on the Air Mobility Command's vision led us to discussing the barriers they were facing in achieving that vision. This is the next step in the strategic process. The most common tools used at this phase of strategy development are the SWOT and PETERS assessments. The SWOT identifies the organization's strengths, weaknesses, opportunities, and threats, while the PETERS identifies potential external barriers of a political, environmental, technological, economic, regulatory, and sociological nature. After the organization has defined these current and potential future impact factors, they can begin to identify the strengths they must leverage and the major barriers they will need to overcome to continue to execute their mission and achieve their vision for the future. Using affinity charts we narrowed these major barriers to a handful from which 3–5 year breakthrough objectives could be stated that if achieved would allow the organization to achieve its vision.

Performing SWOT and PETERS assessments is the *what*. We want to delve a little into the *how*. One mistake that organizations or facilitators make (and we have made in the past) is to conduct these assessments in a joint offsite format. Typically this involves gathering senior leadership and their staff and posing questions that draw out the various elements of the assessment. The problem with doing this in a group setting is that responders tend to be influenced by the leadership, and their frame of mind shifts from their view of things to a "corporate view" that is either politically correct or identifies problem areas they see at the corporate level—not the ones that impact them. The other dynamic that occurs in a group setting is that strong personalities tend to dominate the discussions. While this can be mitigated by tools such as silent brainstorming, it is much more effective to use one-on-one interviews with the key leaders, staff, and others such as union leadership to draw out their thoughts, independent of the group. From there the responses are affinitized and discussed with the senior leader prior to conducting the joint session. The reasons for this are to identify areas of concern within the organization and to set up the senior leader as the owner of the strategic session to follow.

A typical set of questions for the interviews covers the following topics:

1. Understanding their current experience/methodology regarding strategy development and SA&D, what went right and what went wrong, and what they would do differently if given the chance.
2. Developing an understanding of the current culture of the organization. Is the current culture one of problem solving and continuous improvement or one of workarounds and poor response to problems?

3. Developing an understanding of the current customers and markets. What are customer expectations and what percentage of the market do they hold?
4. Developing an understanding of where they stand regarding soft technologies such as management techniques and hard technologies such as equipment and software.
5. Developing an understanding of the capability and problem issues surrounding their workforce, their leadership, their suppliers, and their distribution channels.
6. Developing an understanding of how they identify and launch new products or services.
7. Developing an understanding of the competition and where they stand relative to quality, cost, delivery, and innovation.
8. Developing an understanding of their business structure and how it aligns/supports their value streams— the way their business is aligned to produce value added to their customers and how efficient/effective they are in executing their value added.
9. Developing an understanding of their core competencies, the morale of the organization, whom they hire, and how they train.

Although the questions themselves may vary when tailored to the organization, it is important that the questions be open ended and solicit the flow of information, as opposed to closed ended, allowing for simple answers like yes or no. From the open-ended questions the interviewer has the opportunity to probe further with closed-ended questions to bring out particular areas of concern.

The answers are then affinitized into general focus areas that need addressing through our strategies. These focus areas, as noted in our Air Mobility Command example above, become the foundation for our 3–5 year BTOs.

We discuss the mission, vision, and breakthrough areas with the senior leader to validate our findings. A report is generated to the Strategy Steering Team, and the first group session is established. In that session it is important for the senior leader to be seen as the one driving the discussion. If there are external facilitators, they need to remain facilitators and not invest directly in the discussions.

The first session is used to establish or validate the mission and to gain consensus on the BTOs. We establish or validate the vision for the organization and then open up a discussion on the various scenarios the organization is facing.

Scenario planning is used to identify a handful of most likely future states and the early indicators that a scenario is likely to unfold. Executing a long-range strategy based on today's situation and a desired end state may be the fastest path to a desired vision, but there may be potential future scenarios that if they were to unfold would totally derail that straight-line strategy. By identifying highly potential futures, the organization can develop strategies capable of adjusting to early indicators that reveal that one of those futures is about to unfold. This is accomplished by understanding the current predetermined elements affecting the future, identifying a handful of the most likely future scenarios, and then identifying early indicators that provide a warning that one of the identified future scenarios is about to unfold. This allows adjusting the strategy to a predetermined path before the critical point of the future unfolding. A robust strategy capable of shifting to the potential future is better than the straight-line strategy the organization might execute without the insight provided by scenario planning.

A well-known example of successful scenario planning occurred with Royal Dutch Shell. Royal Dutch Shell used scenario planning in the 1970s to accurately predict the possibility of an oil supply disruption and dramatic increase in prices caused by reduced U.S. oil reserves and the new negotiating power of a less-than-friendly OPEC (Organization of Petroleum Exporting Countries). When war in the Middle East sparked the unfolding of one of their projected futures, the company was able to take advantage by executing their strategy for the unfolding scenario much faster than their competitors. As a result, Royal Dutch Shell was able to capture a significant share of the global oil market.

After the likely futures are defined, we fine-tune our BTOs to ensure that they define overall strategies that are able to adjust to the most likely futures. This leads us to a discussion regarding the limits of our resources and the critical path to attaining our BTOs over the 3–5 year period of strategy execution. From the critical path we establish high AEIPs. Like any schedule, the further out, the looser the plan. As we get closer in, the plans become more firm.

The second session is used to identify the enterprise improvement priorities for the upcoming year of implementation. A key at this point is to identify the key performance metrics by which we will measure our strategic progress. They must have targets that are measurable, quantifiable, and qualitative. They must have a scheduled delivery, and the organization must define the resources they are going to allocate to them. This is often a contentious process in itself, and as such we often assign a subteam to work the metrics issue and report back to the team in the third session. After the Strategic Steering Team settles on the AEIPs, we discuss the catchball process.

The catchball process is critical to gaining commitment on the part of the organization's members. Each of the members takes the AEIPs down to their part of the organization and develops the supporting AIPs that they will contribute in the upcoming year. They identify their parochial requirements and add them to the overall improvement priorities for their segment of the organization. These two often-competing sets of priorities are then bounced up against their resource capability and are trimmed to those objectives they feel they can truly accomplish over the next year. One on one they negotiate their AIPs with the senior leader, who has the option to reorganize their priorities to allocate resources in a manner that best benefits the organization as a whole. This catchball process and development of supporting AIPs is cascaded down to each level of the organization until each of the subordinate organizations has negotiated its portion of the strategic plan for the upcoming year; then the Strategic Steering Team comes back together for the third session.

In the third session each of the members reports on their negotiated AIPs and commitments for the upcoming year. The team as a whole discusses whether the accumulated plans will support the targets set for the AEIPs. If not, then the targets must be adjusted. From there a discussion is opened regarding development of a change management and communications plan. Kotter's 8 Step Process to Leading Change is used as the foundation for the plan. The team hears from the Metrics sub-team and develops the scoring methodology (such as Balanced Scorecard) to track progress. The strategy map is completed, and then the team establishes the cadence or battle rhythm of meetings to report progress at the various levels of the organization. They also complete the governance structure for the time going forward. Typically, the operating level is tracking progress on a daily basis and reporting weekly, the group level is tracking progress weekly and reporting monthly, and the executive level is tracking quarterly.

As noted, the remaining steps of the SA&D process will be discussed in detail in Chapter 6. In the next chapter we will discuss the cultural elements of an organization required to successfully execute and sustain the strategic process.

PART II

Organizational Performance Model

5

Culture and Orientation of the Organization

Driving Strategy to Execution

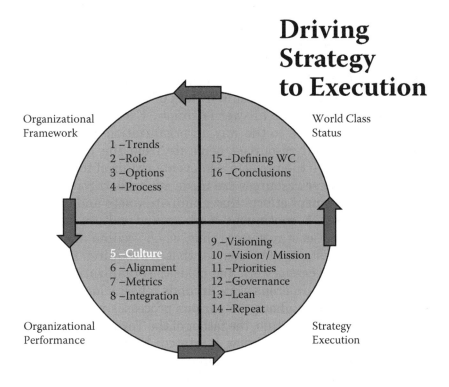

Organizational Framework

1 –Trends
2 –Role
3 –Options
4 –Process

15 –Defining WC
16 –Conclusions

World Class Status

5 –Culture
6 –Alignment
7 –Metrics
8 –Integration

9 –Visioning
10 –Vision / Mission
11 –Priorities
12 –Governance
13 –Lean
14 –Repeat

Organizational Performance

Strategy Execution

The rate of change is not going to slow down anytime soon. If anything, competition in most industries will probably speed up even more in the next few decades.

—John P. Kotter
Leading Change *(Harvard Business Press, 1996, p. 161)*

In an excellent book, *The High-Velocity Edge,* author Steven Spear identifies characteristics that set companies apart and why some organizations get out in front and stay out in front. A key theme of the book is that the successful organizations have a paradigm of problem solving and continuous improvement. The value chain of an organization is only as strong as its weakest link. When organizations have a major failure or breakdown, the assumption is that there was a break in one of the process links, that someone didn't do their job right, or that there was an unusual set of occurrences that predicated the failure. The reality, as pointed out by Spear, is that organizations that do not have a culture of problem solving and allow or even reward work-arounds have weak links throughout their value chain. They are constantly patching problems and performing minor rework. The value chain is subject to failure anytime additional stress is placed on it, and it could come anywhere along the process chain. Why talk of this in a book about strategy execution? The answer is simple. Executing a strategy requires changes to the way an organization operates. It requires additional resources, separate from the day-to-day operation, to drive the projects and events required to execute the strategy. These resources are made available through continuous improvement efforts that eliminate waste and free up those resources. A continuous work-around culture creates many small wastes of resources that, when accumulated, add up to a major waste in the resources that are required to make the inefficient processes work and holds the organization back. Additionally, the numerous work-arounds reflect a lack of truly standard work throughout the various processes in the value chain, and as Taiichi Ohno, the father of the Toyota Production System and Lean as we know it, stated, "Without standard work, there can be no continuous improvement."

Much has been written about value stream mapping (VSM) and value stream analysis. VSM, made popular in Lean circles by Mike Rother and John Shook in *Learning to See*, presented a visual tool for understanding the value stream of an organization. The reason this was and is important is that the direction and orientation of a traditional organization is driven by functional paradigms embedded in its members based on the function they support. This creates stovepipe thinking, where the various functional stovepipes not only focus on their individual function in isolation but look at the mission, vision, and strategic plans of the organization through the lens of their functional glasses. Our traditional education systems are designed to train us to be expert specialists in finance, accounting, operations, engineering, and the like. As such we traditionally organize our business around those functions, setting up departments with heads that are experts in their field. The problem with this is that as individual departments, they focus on what is best for their part of the organization and spend a lot of effort competing for more people, more budget, and better equipment that will allow them to optimally operate their individual function better—often suboptimizing the organization as a whole. Organizations have limited resources, and if they don't apply their resources in a manner that improves the value stream (that function they perform to add value to their customers), they will fall behind their competition, or as is the case with the military and public sector, put a strain on their overall mission capability.

When it comes to executing strategic initiatives, functionaries often define objectives through metrics that tend to be meaningful to their functional organization even though these metrics may be meaningless to the value stream. They believe they are executing the strategy but in truth may be absorbing valuable resources in a manner that actually limits overall strategy execution or drives the various functions in different directions.

Early in his career, one of the authors worked for a major computer and computer peripherals manufacturer. He was in field service and had a team of field service technicians that maintained and repaired products for both internal and external customers. Shortly after he took over a field service branch, the company issued a directive that each branch was to find ways to improve revenues and profits by at least

15 percent over the next 12 months. He began looking at the numbers. The author discovered that he was missing revenues from several of his internal, corporate customers for products his branch was maintaining. He spent the next 6 weeks cleaning up the internal agreements, ensuring that he was getting paid for the internal work. In doing so he was able to increase revenues by 25 percent and raise profits by the increase in revenues, as his branch was already supporting the workload and had no additional expenses. For his efforts the author received a raise, a bonus, and a promotion. But the reality of the situation was that all he was doing was moving money from one part of the organization to another. The net impact was zero, or truth be told, negative, because 6 weeks of time was used to work through the issue, and the result was hundreds of additional transactions and the costs associated with them. He was doing what was best for his department, and he was being judged by metrics that rewarded behavior that was best for his part of the organization, even though it hurt the organization as a whole. The company he worked for was making $3 billion in revenues when he joined them. It no longer exists.

To effectively execute their strategies, organizations need to think in terms of value streams and develop a culture of problem solving and continuous improvement. This often requires business process reengineering (first introduced by Michael Hammer in 1990), physically reorganizing the organization around value streams, or developing virtual value stream teams. It always requires key performance metrics that measure success at the enterprise level and a governance system that measures progress, creates accountability to executing the strategic initiatives, and allows for course corrections should conditions change or progress not meet expectations.

To summarize, a culture of problem solving and continuous improvement, coupled with an orientation focused on the value stream of the organization, ensures that the organization's limited resources are focused on the "true north," or the direction in which the organization's strategy is working to take them. Solving problems and eliminating waste provide the discipline in the system and free up the resources an organization needs to work the projects and events required in executing the strategic plans.

Summary

A clue to the critical path we discussed in Chapter 4 regarding how to establish the proper annual enterprise improvement priorities (AEIPs) lies in building the environmental foundation for change prior to attempting to execute the core strategic plan. If the proper environment for alignment and execution doesn't exist at the time the strategy alignment and deployment (SA&D) is launched, then a significant amount of the first year's SA&D effort should be in developing a culture of disciplined problem solving and continuous improvement while aligning the orientation of the organization in a way that focuses on the value stream of the organization and breaks the paradigms of traditional stovepipe thinking.

6
Strategy Alignment and Deployment/ Strategy Execution

Driving Strategy to Execution

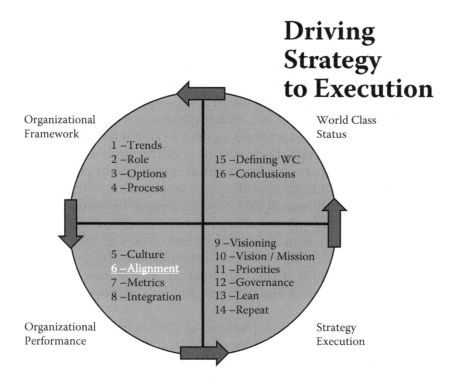

Organizational Framework

1 –Trends
2 –Role
3 –Options
4 –Process

World Class Status

15 –Defining WC
16 –Conclusions

5 –Culture
6 –Alignment
7 –Metrics
8 –Integration

9 –Visioning
10 –Vision / Mission
11 –Priorities
12 –Governance
13 –Lean
14 –Repeat

Organizational Performance

Strategy Execution

Strategy alignment and deployment (SA&D) is the process that converts strategy to action. The *alignment* part ensures that the various elements of the organization are aligned to the overall strategy and have improvement priorities that, when executed, will support the strategic goals and objectives of the organization. The *deployment* part defines those specific activities to be taken by each element of the organization to execute the strategy.

Three critical elements are involved in executing a robust SA&D. Think of it as a three-legged stool. Without all three legs in place, the stool would tip over. It's the same with SA&D.

1. First, a consistent methodology needs to be used throughout the organization. This seems obvious, but we often find that large organizations allow for local options regarding how they execute the overall strategy of the enterprise. We also find that many organizations allow local interpretation of the strategy, or that they are even allowed to disregard the higher strategy altogether in favor of a local strategy. Developing a consistent methodology for the organization as a whole is the first step in aligning the various elements of the organization to an overall strategy deployment.

2. The second element is a robust governance system that requires tracking progress against a critical few key performance metrics. Each overall breakthrough objective (BTO) and corresponding annual improvement priority (AIP) has to have an enterprise-level metric with targets for improvement and implementation milestones.

3. Third, as strategy execution requires change, a change management plan is needed to overcome the inherent resistance to change within an organization. This is especially important if the organization creates new value stream alignment and drives continuous improvement.

As noted in Chapter 3, a plethora of strategic models exist. Having worked with numerous models that were already embedded in organizations, we will describe two models we prefer. In this chapter we will describe a model based on Hoshin Kanri, with elements of the Balanced Scorecard that work well, integrating the discipline of a robust deployment methodology with a focus on key perspectives, metrics, and dashboards to track progress. In the chapters contained in Part III, "Executing the Strategy," we will delve further into a model utilizing visioning and scenario modeling, along with a strategy mapping methodology. We present these two methodologies to show that although there are multiple strategic models to choose from, the success or failure of strategic planning is determined by the linkage of strategy development to strategy execution—combining the consistent methodology with a strong governance plan and a method of dealing with resistance to change.

Hoshin Kanri was developed in Japan by integrating the work of W. Edwards Deming and Joseph M. Juran with management by objectives (MBO) elements out of Peter Drucker's *The Practice of Management*. The Japanese words *hoshin kanri* loosely translate into "controlling the compass needle," or managing the direction of an organization to a specific goal. *The Balanced Scorecard*, by Robert S. Kaplan and David P. Norton, reinforces the Plan-Do-Check-Act nature of the process by providing focus on the four key perspectives of financial, customer, internal processes, and learning and growth, along with the development of a scorecard that is used to track progress and support the governance system.

Figure 6.1 describes the SA&D model being discussed in this chapter. It determines the present situation through a series of interviews with various members of the leadership and tests the organization's vision, reiterating their BTOs. It then develops a Balanced Scorecard strategy map, providing a visual representation of the key initiatives and the metrics associated with them. This is where the shift from strategy to execution begins in the forming of AEIPs. One of the key mistakes organizations make in their strategy execution is to develop their long-range objectives and initiate their strategy execution without recognizing that they have limited resources and that human nature is to deal with the urgent over the important. Because the goals are anywhere from 3 to 5 years out, they delay action, so people think that there is plenty of time to work toward the strategic goals next month, or even next year.

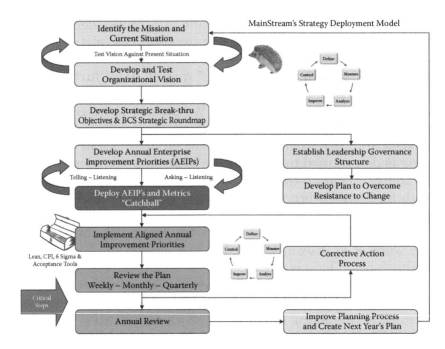

Figure 6.1 SA&D model.

The discipline of the SA&D model requires us to take our longer range BTOs and look at the critical path to strategic implementation. Then we break those long-range strategic plans down into AEIPs that are bounced against the critical path to success as well as available resources. These AEIPs are further broken down into quarterly and even monthly objectives. But before we set these AEIPs we conduct a critical process to ensure that we have not only alignment but also buy-in throughout the organization. This is accomplished through *catchball*. As previously noted in Chapter 4, in catchball we send our AEIP plans down to the next level of the organization and ask that level to develop their supporting annual improvement priorities (AIPs). During this process, they get to include their local priorities and to challenge and modify the higher level expectations based on their real-world constraints and knowledge of conditions. They negotiate the balance of local to corporate priorities and commitments with higher leadership. Higher leadership has the option to deselect local priorities if need be, until a plan is agreed to between the two levels of the

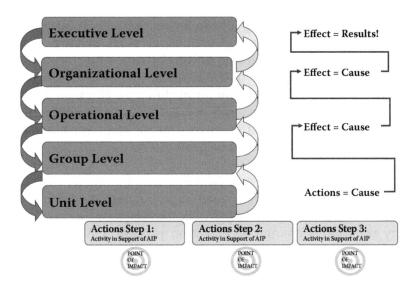

Figure 6.2 Cascading.

organization. Catchball goes back and forth with each level of the organization until there is a consistent and aligned set of strategic AIPs and action plans at the actionable levels of the organization that are committed to throughout the organization. Figure 6.2 shows how this cascading works.

Each AIP at every level of the organization must have a primary champion and assigned resources as well as defined metrics and implementation/improvement targets, along with monthly milestones. These are reviewed on a periodic basis, depending on where in the organization they are being tracked. A typical battle rhythm is to track daily or weekly at the lowest actionable levels of the organization, monthly at the group or operational levels, and quarterly at the organizational or executive levels. In each case the various levels of the organization report status to the next level in the hierarchy and are held accountable for executing their plans and achieving their milestone objectives. At each of these levels corrective action is taken in the event of a miss. In the past, much of this tracking and presenting was a result of extensive manual tracking; but more recently, with the advent of software-assisted programs, organizations rely on automated dashboards to provide real-time status at the various levels of the organization. This real-time status reporting allows for more timely intervention in the event that things slip or metrics start driving in the wrong direction. Because it is driven by rolled up raw data, it also avoids any "gaming" of the reports.

This tracking of status, accountability to the next higher level of the organization, and corrective action process provides the governance that ensures that the strategic plans are being implemented with the desired effects.

The third element of a successful SA&D we noted relates to overcoming the natural resistance to change through change management. Again, there are many noted methodologies for managing change. Early in the development of our company we used a change acceleration process (CAP) that was developed by Dr. Noel Tichy for Jack Welch when he was chief executive officer of General Electric. More recently we have adapted the 8 Step model developed by John Kotter in his book *Leading Change.*

Step 1 recognizes that change is hard and that people will accept change only if they understand the need or urgency to change. It is incumbent on leadership to define the need for change. Again, this seems rather obvious, but because various leaders in the organization have varying paradigms based on the priorities and needs of their individual departments or functions, their view of the need for change varies. Before executing a strategic initiative that requires change, the leadership has to come together and get on the same page so that the message is consistent throughout the organization.

The second step is to develop a guiding coalition for the change. Adapting a consistent methodology for SA&D, complete with a governance system, helps to establish that coalition.

The third step, identify a vision for what the change will result in, is accomplished in the strategic planning session, but it is Step 4 where many organizations fail.

Step 4 is to communicate the vision to all levels of the organization. We can't tell you how many times we have worked with senior levels of an organization in developing the need for change and a vision for the future, only to have that message die one level down in the organizational chain of command. As most change is executed from the bottom up in organizations, it is critical that every member of the organization understand not only the need for implementing the strategic initiatives, but also what the vision for the future holds—both if the organization is successful and if it fails.

Step 5 is to remove obstacles. Aside from establishing clear goals and expectations and providing the workforce with the tools, training, and resources to do what we are asking them to do, removing barriers is one of the three key responsibilities of leadership.

The sixth step in Kotter's process is to create short-term wins. This helps to create excitement and sends the message that the process is working.

The seventh step is to build on the change and leverage the short-term wins to accelerate the change process.

Step 8 is to anchor the change in corporate culture. This requires establishing new standard work around the change and monitoring things to prevent slippage back into the old ways.

This element of change management is one of the reasons why most organizations require outside help for their first few iterations of SA&D.

Change experts note that in any distribution of people, a small number of individuals are early adapters willing to accept change, and an equal number are active resisters to change. The remaining individuals are somewhere on the fence (Figure 6.3).

Transitioning an organization to a desired state requires overcoming the resistance to change. Getting momentum and transforming the thoughts and actions of individuals involves

Most Organizations Need Help to Overcome the Resistance to Change

Figure 6.3 Resistance to change.

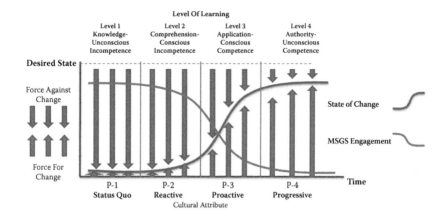

Figure 6.4 Levels of learning.

learning. As the organization's members learn the value of the desired change and begin to understand the reasons and need for changes in process, they begin to join the early adapters.

Because of this distribution of early adapters and shifts in learning, we can define transition to a changed state as one of overcoming the inherent resistance over time, and relating it to an organization's levels of learning (Figure 6.4).

Level 1—Client organization, as a whole, is "unconsciously incompetent." They are status quo in their thinking and do not see the need for change. There are a few members of the leadership who are committed to the desired change, but as a whole the organization doesn't know what it doesn't know. The organization lacks the perceived value to desire and contribute to the change.

Level 2—Client organization is "consciously incompetent." They see the need for change and are reactive in their approach and use of continuous process improvement (CPI) tools and methods to tactically solve problems. There is momentum building in support of change. The organization is aware that it has problems it needs to overcome but is unsure how to overcome or avoid problems.

Level 3—The organization as a whole is "consciously competent." They are proactive, using the tools and methods in a strategic manner to avoid problems. They know what the problems are, and they consciously know what tools they need to apply to overcome those problems.

Level 4—The client organization is at a level of "unconscious competence." They are progressive in their thinking. They know what to do and do it without consciously thinking about it. It is embedded into their cultural mindset.

The level of support and the kind of support clients need throughout this transition change as the client's organization shifts between the various levels of learning. Because of this, the consulting organization must apply situational consulting, based on where the client is in that transition.

In Chapter 4 we discussed a process for developing an organization's strategy. These were Steps 1–4 of the strategy development and SA&D process that supports this recommended strategy deployment model.

Step 5 of the process requires each of the organization's layers to develop the execution plans, complete with projects and events required to achieve their AIP targets. These plans are set into a project management format, and progress is tracked at each of the key milestones. Lean and Six Sigma implementation teams are established and progress is tracked on a continuous basis, communicating up and down the organizational chain on achievements. Throughout this process the leadership is executing various levels of Kotter's 8 Step Process to Leading Change, reiterating the case for change, the vision, removing obstacles, creating early wins, leveraging those wins to increase the rate of improvement, and anchoring the change into new standardized work, enforcing discipline within the new systems and structures.

Step 6 is to vigorously follow the governance structure and track progress on the weekly, monthly, and quarterly review schedule, using those meetings to remove barriers and develop corrective actions.

Step 7 is to conduct root cause analysis when plans slip and to apply solutions, including additional resources if required.

Step 8 is to conduct an annual review and collect lessons learned.

Step 9 is to prepare for the next year's plan, addressing shortfalls and new requirements.

Summary

Throughout this process it is important to stay on course to the overall 3–5 year plan AIPs. Avoid the "groundhog day" mistake of reinventing the strategic plan each year. With each new year the organization adds a new year to the 5-year plan, thus making it a rolling strategy and SA&D. Remember that most organizations require several iterations (years) of execution to become proficient in the SA&D process. Those that stick with it and continue to learn reap the rewards of achieving their goals and objectives.

7

Organizational Performance Measures

Driving Strategy to Execution

Organizational Framework

1 –Trends
2 –Role
3 –Options
4 –Process

World Class Status

15 –Defining WC
16 –Conclusions

5 –Culture
6 –Alignment
7 –Metrics
8 –Integration

9 –Visioning
10 –Vision / Mission
11 –Priorities
12 –Governance
13 –Lean
14 –Repeat

Organizational Performance

Strategy Execution

Too many people prefer the misery of uncertainty over the pain of change.

In the Gobi desert there is a regiment of troops. Their primary function is to keep the railroad tracks clear of sand. The purpose of the railroad is to deliver food and supplies to the troops. Does this seem strange? Eliminating the regiment would eliminate the need for the railroad and therefore the need to deliver food and supplies.

Often we become comfortable doing things the way they have always been done, never questioning why. Like soldiers in the Gobi desert, traditional measurement systems (such as labor efficiency or productivity measures) not only are ineffective, but they are usually a waste, and they are often destructive.

In a recent meeting, one of the authors encountered an extremely frustrated U.S. Air Force two-star general. In his own words he stated: "Over the last year we have executed dozens of process improvement events. However, I can't prove to anyone that anything is better. No one has bothered to track any performance metrics that demonstrate that anything has actually improved. I don't want any more improvements executed unless there are metrics assigned that will demonstrate that we have been successful."

In designing a strategy we soon learn that it is impossible to execute a meaningful strategy without incorporating some measures of performance. These are needed for several reasons:

- Validation of process improvements
- Employee motivation
- Goal achievement

In this chapter we will consider some of the critical elements of a successful measurement system. We will start with a review of the measurement–motivation relationship. This will be followed with a discussion of several measurement options. The chapter will end with a comparison of the various measurement methodologies and how they relate to a strategic system.

The Measurement–Motivation Relationship

The authors feel that the key to successful performance in any strategic system is not in the procedures. Rather, successful strategy performance is achieved by establishing meaningful structured measurement systems focused on results. With this idea in mind, Gerhard Plenert received an American Production and Inventory Control Society (APICS) grant for research focused on the relationship between motivation and measurement,* with the belief that—

> The measurement system directly affects employee performance.

The author conducted surveys and interviews and eventually experimented with a test case. He went to work for Precision Printers, Inc. (PPI), a company that was structured and focused on volume. Quality was treated as secondary in importance. However, the company's poor performance in quality had dragged it into the red (nonprofitable). It was not used as a measure of employee performance. A shift was made to eliminate the volume measure and focus on quality performance. The foundation of the belief was that, as in riding a bicycle, you first need to learn how to balance (quality); then you can learn to go faster (volume). However, the reverse is not true; going fast will not help you to learn balance. The transition from volume to quality occurred as a series of stages over about 6 months:

- Strategy workshop used to identify and align strategy to operational performance
- Production planning training
- Quality management training
- Goal/measurement system redesign

---

* The details of this research were published in an APICS (American Production and Inventory Control Society) Education and Research Foundation Study, "Performance Measurement Systems and How They Are Used As Employee Motivators," 7/1999, #07022. A summary was published in *APICS—The Performance Advantage*, February 1999, as a guest editorial by Gerhard Plenert. Additional detail on the motivation–measurement relationship was published in the *Production and Inventory Management Journal* in late 2000.

- Quality Week
- Team-based empowerment
- Ongoing continuous improvement programs

PPI realized that the volume- and revenue-based performance measurement system was driving throughput but not quality. The measurement transformation that occurred at PPI was to take out the volume- and revenue-based measurement system. The company had built up $1 million worth of unshipped customized finished goods inventory because the measurement system focused on revenue produced. If it was produced, it counted as manufactured revenue, even if it never shipped. The measurement transformation that took place changed the focus of the company to quality units delivered to the customer. It was no longer advantageous to produce inventory. Inventory levels were limited to no more than 30 days.

The measurement change process started by implementing an extensive training program that focused on production and inventory management techniques. The training focused on how inventory buildup was destroying profitability. It showed that managing inventory was more important for profitability than managing labor. It also demonstrated that quality could improve only if it was measured and motivated by an incentive program. The current defect rate was costing the company money and chewed up valuable capacity. It taught the employees about how quality should be measured and that quality improvements come from the employees, not from management. Quality management training was also included. This training focused on cross-functional team building with empowered ownership.

The next phase of the program required a point in time where the old measurement system was officially out and the new system was in place. This implementation point was set up as Quality Week. During this week the goal was to produce only perfect parts. The employees were given the freedom to tear anything apart, move anything, or team up with anyone. The golden rule of the entire exercise was, "It doesn't matter if only one part is produced, but that part has to be perfect."

Next, PPI had to construct some new goals and objectives. Quality was the new goal and was defined as

- Defect rate reduction
- Customer complaint reduction
- Improved delivery performance
- Cycle time reduction
- Inventory level reduction

All of these measures have a direct effect on profitability and customer satisfaction.

Quality Week began with a great deal of fear and trepidation. Management was concerned that the employees would just stand around, not knowing what to do. However, what happened was just the opposite. Most of the employees were excited. They had always wanted to have the time and freedom to attack the machinery and figure out why failures happened and how they could be fixed. Teams formed spontaneously. Management basically had to get out of the way or else get run over. The employees were enjoying the experience, and several of them commented about how much fun they were having. The Quality Week program taught the employees about teaming, goal setting, and empowerment. At first some were skeptical, but when they saw the rewards for their performance, they became intensely involved in the process of improvement.

The total transformation from volume to quality took about 8 months. The first 3 months were spent in preparation for the shift to quality (Quality Week), and the last 5 months were focused on the implementation of the transition. Some of the measurable results can be seen in Figures 7.1 to 7.5. Figure 7.1 shows how the defect rate was steadily increasing from May 1997 to October 1997. Then there was a shift, both in the direction of the trend and in the level of the defects. This figure demonstrates the dramatic effect of the change in measurement methods.

Some additional figures show that the impact of the changing metrics had rippling effects throughout the organization. For example, Figure 7.2 records customer complaints and shows how they were decreasing because of the new emphasis on quality. Figure 7.3 shows that on-time shipment performance also improved in that there were fewer late shipments. This is directly related to Figure 7.4, which shows how quality improvements directly reduced cycle times. All these

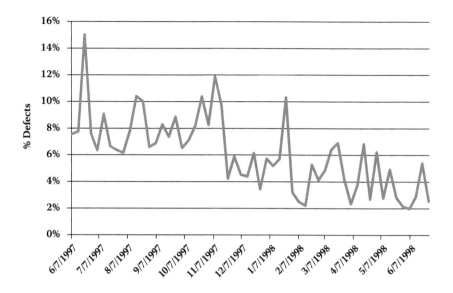

Figure 7.1 Defect rates.

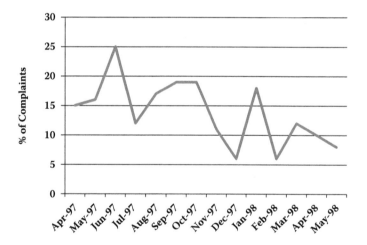

Figure 7.2 Complaints.

improvements are linked together, including the performance of FGI (finished goods inventory) in Figure 7.5, which has been steadily going down. Cycle time reductions reduced lead times, which made the organization more responsive to customer demands. Cycle time reductions also improved on-time

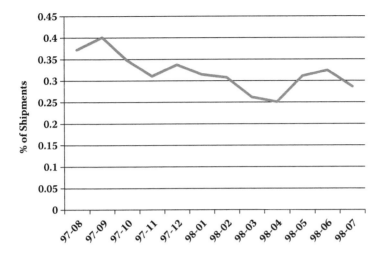

Figure 7.3 Shipments not on time.

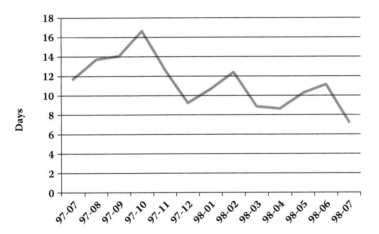

Figure 7.4 Cycle time.

performance. And all these performance efficiencies were triggered by a measurement system modification.

One of the most significant impacts that affected the entire plant was that the collection of efficiencies generated an overall 20 percent increase in capacity. This had an enormous impact on the organization's ability to generate additional revenue. The overall effect of what seems like one small change

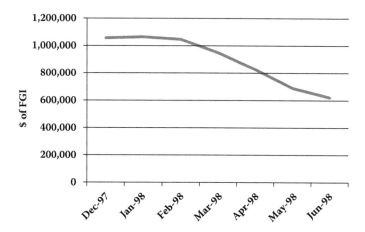

Figure 7.5 Finished goods inventory (FGI).

(changing the measurement system) resulted in taking the company from red to black in profitability.

Some interesting, nonmeasurable, and self-motivated results of the shift in measurement system to a quality measurement process (these are nonmeasurable but they have overall measurable improvements in total performance) include the following:

- A strong shift from departmentalization to interdepartmental efforts
- Engineers working on the production floor
- Spontaneous teams organized to solve specific problems
- A shift in company culture to being "one big family"
- Greatly improved communication
- Greatly improved customer relations

The PPI measurement–motivation research case example demonstrates how integrated the measurement–motivation relationship is. Some additional findings of the overall research project (taken from the APICS Education and Research Foundation Working Paper) are as follows:

First, corporate vision and mission statements (goals) tend to have very little to do with the measurement systems. Tradition has more influence on the measurement methodologies than do goals. For example, a company has slogans and banners all over the facility promoting customer-oriented quality, but employees are still measured and paid incentive pay based on the number of units produced. These employees care very little about quality, since spending more time checking quality will directly reduce the amount of their paychecks. This is fundamentally wrong. Strategy should define the measurement environment and not be abstracted from it.

Second, financial measures promote short-term thinking. Financial measures cause managers to be numbers-focused and will do anything to make the numbers look good for the short term. Long-term investments are discouraged since they negatively affect the short-term numbers by increasing debt and costs. The result is that a "fix and patch" strategy wins out over a "replace with newer/improved technology" strategy because it costs less for the short term.

Third, blanket corporate office–dictated international measurement systems don't reflect the local management style or culture and are often de-motivating rather than motivating. One interesting example occurred at a plant in Mexico where the incentive pay system was introduced in an attempt to make employees work faster. The result was that in this culture employees looked at money as a means to giving them more family time. Additional income meant that they could work less hours. In the end, the incentive pay system increased the absentee rate, which wasn't the desired result. It should be noted that not all areas of Mexico work the same way. This result was specific to the author's location in Mexico.

Fourth, measurement systems are often thought of as data collection systems, and all data is considered to be a good thing. For example, after running statistical process control (SPC) for one year, one company contacted the author requesting some recommendations on what should be done with all the data. When the author told them to throw it out since SPC is a process tool for continuous improvement, not for data collection, they were very frustrated. The data is only valuable for current process optimization, not for historical purposes. Excessive data is often a waste (refer to the seven wastes of Lean) when it serves no value-adding purpose.

Fifth, there seems to be no understanding of the relationship between goal achievement and resource efficiency. For example, in most discrete manufacturing, labor is less than

10 percent of the value-added product content, and materials comprise over 50 percent. Yet, when cost-cutting measures are enacted, we still tend to focus more on the 10 percent and tend to ignore the 50+ percent. One company increased labor productivity by 10 percent (employee throughput) at the cost of decreased materials efficiency (lower inventory turns) by 5 percent (increased labor efficiency required more materials availability). Simple mathematics shows us that the increased labor efficiency increased profits by 1 percent overall (10 percent times 10 percent), and that decreased materials efficiency hurt profits by 2.5 percent overall (50 percent times 5 percent). Therefore, increased labor productivity cost the company a 1.5 percent reduction in overall profitability.

Now that we understand that a measurement system is critical to motivating the proper response from our employees, let's take a look at what measurement options exist.

Measurement

Socrates told people what to do and they killed him for it.

This chapter has been dedicated to a discussion of measurement simply because it's the most common area in which strategic mistakes are made. For example, everyone has heard the story of the plant manager who attempted to follow "Lean manufacturing" principles (run the plant with no wasted resources), only to approach getting fired because inventory reductions had destroyed his short-term financial "current ratios." The month following his chastisement, he repurchased the inventory. Similarly, there is the story of the plant that had one of the best quality systems available. It had statistical process control (SPC), total quality control (TQC), total quality management (TQM) banners, Six Sigma programs, ISO (International Organization for Standardization) certification, quality control (QC) circles, and more. However, the plant was being closed because of poor quality. The author was invited into the plant to discuss why quality was so poor in spite of all the installed systems. The answer was simple: The company was measuring performance and paying bonuses based on throughput through the work center. The evaluation systems stressed throughput, and no matter how much hype was given to quality, throughput made the difference between an employee getting fired and getting more pay. This brings us to an important measurement principle:

> Increasing quality does not ensure increased competitiveness; it may decrease it!

> Increasing productivity does not guarantee increased profits; it may actually decrease profitability!

Intuitively, this does not seem correct, because our training has taught us that increasing productivity and quality is a good thing. However, increasing productivity and quality in the wrong areas reduces the performance efficiency in other areas.[*] Let's take a look at some of the measures of performance that are available.

Customer Quality

World class customer satisfaction requires that the customer becomes central in the manufacturing planning and scheduling process. However, for customer quality to exist, it first needs to be redefined. Traditional definitions of quality revolve around the ISO definition of quality, which focuses on meeting or exceeding engineering standards. However, Japanese methodologies like concept management stress that quality needs to be redefined as "delighting a customer."

> A delighted customer is one who is so excited by and attached to a product as to be automatically and unconsciously attracted to it.
> The excited customer is at the point where he or she will select a product based on emotion, and not simply based on logic.

---

[*] Parts of this section are taken from the book *Making Innovation Happen: Concept Management through Integration,* by Gerhard Plenert and Shozo Hibino (Boca Raton, FL: St. Lucie Press, 1998).

For customer quality to exist, we want to measure and motivate customer delight. To do this, we need to interact with the customers and find out what delights them. The product team that is responsible for a specific product needs to find out what it is that generates this delight. Satisfaction is not sufficient. And the team also needs to realize that the definition of delight changes over time. It can't be discovered once and then be expected to remain the same. It is a constantly changing target.

An excellent book on quality is Ken Shelton's *In Search of Quality*, which lists the opinions of 43 industrial leaders on what quality should be, including the CEOs of world class companies and quality leaders like Deming, Juran, and Crosby. These statements should not be considered the last word on quality. Rather, they should be considered a benchmark we should all be ready to beat.

Productivity Thinking and Value-Added Thinking

Productivity has long been a measure of performance. However, traditional productivity measures in the United States have focused on labor productivity, ignoring other elements of the productivity equation. Blindly focusing on labor productivity as a measure of success can result in a loss of profitability. Rather, what we need to focus on is "thinking productivity."

Do the right things before you do things right.

Thinking productivity is where we look at the entire value-added content of the product and measure productivity based on the product's full content. Thinking productivity challenges the way we do things. It questions the purpose of all activities. For example, the purpose of data collection is not for cost accounting but rather for motivation. If data collection is not generating the appropriate response from the factory and its resources, then it is a waste. All resources throughout the organization should receive a similar evaluation.

Benchmarking

Benchmarking is where we compare ourselves with others, both inside and outside of our industry sector. Benchmarking institutes exist throughout the world, tabulating and analyzing financial and operational data about companies and grouping this data into industrial sectors. For example, the American Productivity and Quality Group (APQG) in Houston, Texas, has a benchmarking institute that offers benchmarking services. Additionally, directories like Dun & Bradstreet's Key Business Ratios and the Supply Chain Council's SCOR model provide additional sources for benchmarking ratios.

There are two types of benchmarking—internal benchmarking and external benchmarking. External benchmarking is where we compare ourselves with others that are in the same or similar industries. A key principle in external benchmarking is

- As long as you're playing catch-up, the best you can ever get is caught up, and that's just not good enough.
- Or, stated another way, copying your competitor won't help you beat your competitor. You need to think beyond your competitor.

If you're behind in the race, external benchmarking can be very valuable. But if you're trying to be leading edge, external benchmarking can cause complacency.

Internal benchmarking is where you compare your performance against yourself, either between departments or the same department against itself over time. Internal benchmarking is a continuous improvement measurement tool that motivates change. It's the way the Japanese developed Just in Time (JIT) over a 30-year period. They were the best, so the only way they could get better was by internal examination.

How Should We Measure?

Like all elements of an organization, measurement systems should be continuously receptive to change. We need to define, redefine, and re-redefine our measurement system as the organization changes. This includes a move toward an FCS (finite capacity scheduling) environment. We need to focus the measurement system on the redefined organizational purpose. Additionally, we need to—

Focus on the purpose of the numbers, not on the numbers themselves!

Conventional methods focus on measuring the speed of accomplishment. Rather, we should focus on the effectiveness of the accomplishment or on the long-term value of the accomplishment.

Resources flow toward what is measured.

—Tom Tuttle

If we are measuring short-term improvements, our resources, including the human resource and its efforts, will focus on improvements in the short term. Therefore, if we want long-term improvements like customer quality, then we need long-term measures. In the United States the automotive industry has still not converted its plants to JIT production methods. This JIT transition hasn't occurred because everyone, from the CEO on down, is measured on short-term performance measures, and a conversion to JIT is an extremely long-term project. Who cares if it is beneficial to the consumer (higher levels of quality and lower costs of operation in JIT) or to the long-term stability and even existence of the company (vis-à-vis competition)? What's most important is that everyone, from the CEO on down, must satisfy the needs of the measurement system so that they can "keep their job and get a raise," which is ultimately the goal of all employees.

Measurement systems are strategic. They require long-term thinking. Organizations will resist moving to something long term because they fear that the short-term measures will be disappointing. The answer lies in reevaluating the strategic goals of the organization to assure ourselves that we have a world class focus of growth for our organization.

Summary

A friend of mine has a son who was somewhat familiar with construction equipment, having spent a fair bit of time on construction sites. Cement trucks have a beeper that goes off when they back up to warn anyone behind them of potential danger. One day, while in line at a grocery store with his mom, he was standing behind a rather large lady wearing a beeper. Suddenly the beeper went off and the small boy excitedly yelled out, "Watch out! She's going to back up!" He was simply adapting a familiar measurement system to a new situation.

> If you do what you always did,
> you get what you always got.

Avoid getting caught in a rut of applying old measurement methods to our new strategic environment. Staying in the rut may result in a new system giving us old results. Rather, we need to reevaluate what it is that we are trying to accomplish. We need to look closely at our goals and consider what response it is that we are trying to motivate. And we need to consider the measurement options to make sure that the measure we select drives a strategic success.

8

An Integrated
Strategic Model

**Driving
Strategy
to Execution**

Organizational
Framework

World Class
Status

1 –Trends
2 –Role
3 –Options
4 –Process

15 –Defining WC
16 –Conclusions

5 –Culture
6 –Alignment
7 –Metrics
8 –Integration

9 –Visioning
10 –Vision / Mission
11 –Priorities
12 –Governance
13 –Lean
14 –Repeat

Organizational
Performance

Strategy
Execution

As mentioned early on, the main reasons that organizations fail to execute their strategic plans are (1) they treat strategic planning as a once-a-year activity, separate from their day-to-day operation; and (2) after the strategic plan is completed it typically goes on a bookshelf while everyone, albeit vaguely attempting to live up to the expectations of the plan, gets back to the urgent matters that were slipping past as they supported the offsite strategic plan session. It is a classic case of the urgent overriding the important.

The various elements of culture, alignment, and metrics, along with governance, which we will discuss in Chapter 12, are key factors in integrating strategy alignment and deployment into the daily life of the organization. To instill discipline into the system, leadership must develop a certain level of leader standard work (LSW). Much like the standard work performed by members of a Lean organization, leader standard work involves the leader performing routine functions in a systematic and repeatable way. Following are some benefits of LSW:

- Eliminates guesswork for managers and leaders
- Stabilizes the leader's day
- Identifies what leaders should *not* be doing
- Allows routine things to be taken care of with less mental energy, leaving leaders free to focus on making changes and improvements
- Requires discipline

In LSW, leaders will do the following:

- Scrutinize the current situation based on visual controls where possible
- Focus on gaps revealed between expected progress and actual progress
- Hold people accountable to—
  - Complete assigned improvement tasks.
  - Address and close gaps.

Some of the behaviors required to create LSW are as follows:

- Disciplined adherence to process—accountability
  - Set clear expectations.
  - Use regular processes to track completion.
  - Hold employees accountable for assigned tasks and schedules.

- Project management orientation
  - Establish milestones with timelines and targets.
  - Conduct periodic reviews.
  - Establish corrective actions.
- Lean thinking (look for the sources of problems)
  - Apply DMAIC problem-solving discipline (define, measure, analyze, improve, control).
  - Utilize Six Sigma statistical tools where needed to reduce or eliminate variation.
- Balance between production and management systems: Systems must be established to sustain and extend the gains from technical Lean and Six Sigma implementations. A balance must also be struck between day-to-day execution and execution of strategic plans.
- Effective relations between support groups: Leadership must break down the functional stovepipe barriers to value stream management by setting value stream–focused metrics and targets and utilizing cross-functional teams in developing improvement projects aligned to the strategic goals and objectives identified in the SA&D.

To establish the culture we discussed in Chapter 5, leadership must assess and address gaps in the various attributes of a culture of problem solving and continuous improvement (Figure 8.1).

To establish the "battle rhythm" of LSW, avoid trying to establish a rote set of behaviors based on prescribed areas of focus. Instead, conduct an assessment of how well leadership supports the establishment of these attributes as well as how effective they are at the following:

- Providing clear goals and expectations regarding both the day-to-day operational expectations and the expectations regarding the execution of strategic initiatives.
- Providing the workforces with the tools, training, and resources they need both to conduct the day-to-day operation of their job and to execute strategic initiatives.
- Removing the barriers that are constantly getting in the way of successfully achieving both tactical goals and expectations and well as strategic goals and expectations.

Figure 8.1 Culture of problem solving.

Conduct "Day in the Life" reviews of how leaders at various levels of the organization spend their day and determine the changes that are needed to refocus their efforts on limiting their involvement in nonsupport activities to only those critical few that are necessary to maintain the business. An all-too-true "catch-22" of leadership is that most leaders spend more time defending or explaining their level of effectiveness than they do taking action to improve it. As a result, they do not effectively lead, and results in both tactical and strategic execution suffer. This in turn results in spending more time defending or explaining their level of ineffectiveness.

As a member of the senior staff of a computer accessories manufacturing and repair company, this author can remember being in daily 3-hour staff meetings in which the executive vice president would begin the meeting by going around to each of the staff members and assigning new problems he wanted solved. He did this to ensure that he would get those on the table before meeting time ran out. Once he got these out, he would go back and get a status on where each of the staff members were in solving previously assigned problems. Unfortunately, by the time he got back to me so much time had passed that he was often asking me for status on problems he had just assigned me earlier in the meeting. While this seems almost comical, the reality is that even when what would appear to be reasonable time is given to work problems and drive strategic initiatives, most leadership goes from one status meeting to another throughout their week. By the time the week is over and they are back in their next round of meetings, they still haven't had any time to actually provide guidance and work the issues of the day. In effect, they suffer the same fate I suffered under my unreasonable executive vice president.

LSW is the tool leaders use to change that equation by establishing a schedule of activities designed to focus on closing the gaps in their ability to support their team both in their daily operations and their execution of strategic initiatives. Again, we stress that every organization is different, and as such, their LSW should vary. The following example of an LSW layout was developed for one of MainStream GS's Air Force client's in a production environment and provides an example of what LSW might look like.

Element and Description

Daily/Weekly Post Milestone or Daily Operations Plan Review

A formal vehicle exists to review plan vs. actual daily and weekly in a structured manner

The vehicle includes multiple management levels of the organization as well as representatives of production and production support

Information is visible on the production floor (milestones, plan vs. actuals, etc.)

Monthly Key Performance Indicator (KPI)/Metric Reviews (Production and Production Support)

A formal vehicle exists in the organization to review KPIs and metrics on at least a monthly basis (production and production support)

KPIs and metrics are developed to cover quality, cost, delivery, safety, and culture (semblance of Balanced Scorecard approach)

KPIs and metrics are validated using the SMART acronym (specific, measureable, achievable, realistic, and timely)

KPI and metric structure demonstrates alignment of support functions and production to the overall organization level KPIs (no suboptimized silos)

Continued

Continuous Process Improvement (CPI)
(AFSO21, RIE, Enterprise-Level Projects, etc.)

CPI is driven based on strategy deployment and or in response to daily execution opportunities/trends identified via assessment of the current operating system, enterprise level value stream mapping efforts, identified daily systemic operations related opportunities and in direct support of strategy deployment

Business cases exist to support CPI efforts and help provide visibility on ROI, risk mitigation and or net value stream impact

CPI efforts occur at all levels of the organization and within all functional responsibilities (not relegated to only the lower levels of the hierarchical structure)

CPI initiatives follow the tenets of AFSO21 as well as the local requirements of the center (CPIMT, etc.) as required

Squadron Corporate Board (SCB) and Escalation Plan (EP)

Squadron Corporate Board exists and is effective (physically exists and is in accordance with wing requirement), and covers strategy deployment, configuration change management, CPI and Balanced Scorecard review, etc.

Escalation process exists and is effective:
- Issue/opportunity identification and criteria to move from first-line through SCB fully defined and understood
- Process, roles, and responsibilities fully defined and understood

CPI efforts are directly related to and prioritized in accordance with maximizing achievement of strategic objectives and or operational excellence

Meetings

Organization has regularly scheduled meetings concerning the review, status, and path forward of the operation (e.g., production meeting, PMR, production board, MRB, etc.)

Meetings are run via standard work (meeting scope sheet defining meeting description, objectives, agenda, frequency, time, required attendees, etc.)

Meetings are effective (timely, agenda and decision driven, etc.) and contain elements that drive operational excellence and good business decisions

Strategy Deployment

Strategy deployment plans at center, wing, group, and squadron levels
  exist and are effective and align to one another

Tier-down methodology (standard work) is in place to ensure strategic
  alignment of squadron to group to wing to center strategies as well as a
  process for internally managing strategy deployment efforts

CPI efforts properly link to and directly support the local strategy
  deployment plan

Summary

What it comes down to is that to effectively integrate strategy
alignment and deployment into the daily fiber of the organization, the organization must change the way they execute. This
change begins with leadership changing their paradigms of
what their roles and responsibilities are, and it ends with their
changing the manner in which they spend their days so that
the bulk of their time is supporting and affecting the goals and
objectives they desire to achieve.

In Part III we will lay out a robust methodology for defining an organization's strategy and driving it to execution. In
Part IV, within Chapter 15 we will provide an assessment
tool that will further help leaders define the attributes of high
performance in terms of the urgency, empowerment, communications, learning, and discipline that balance day-to-day operational improvement with strategy alignment and deployment.

PART III

Executing the Strategy

9

Visioning/
Scenario Modeling

Driving Strategy to Execution

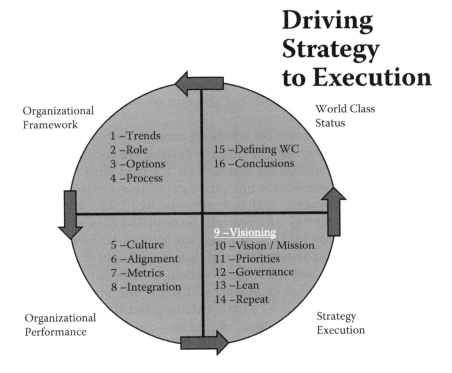

Organizational Framework

World Class Status

1 –Trends
2 –Role
3 –Options
4 –Process

15 –Defining WC
16 –Conclusions

5 –Culture
6 –Alignment
7 –Metrics
8 –Integration

9 –Visioning
10 –Vision / Mission
11 –Priorities
12 –Governance
13 –Lean
14 –Repeat

Organizational Performance

Strategy Execution

It is not the critic who counts: not the man who points out how the strong man stumbles or where the doer of deeds could have done better. The credit belongs to the man who is actually in the arena, whose face is marred by dust and sweat and blood, who strives valiantly, who errs and comes up short again and again, because there is no effort without error or shortcoming, but who knows the great enthusiasms, the great devotions, who spends himself for a worthy cause; who, at the best, knows, in the end, the triumph of high achievement, and who, at the worst, if he fails, at least he fails while daring greatly, so that his place shall never be with those cold and timid souls who knew neither victory nor defeat.

—Theodore Roosevelt

This chapter explains some of the prework that needs to be done as part of a successful and complete long-term strategic planning process. In this chapter we will discuss visioning and scenario modeling. These tools are critical if your strategic perspective looks out 5 years, 10 years, 20 years, or more. It is not that valuable if your perspective is 3 years or less. Unfortunately, the authors have worked with organizations that have a short-term, limited time perspective and don't care what happens beyond 3 years. And in these cases, visioning and scenario planning do not serve a valuable purpose. For this chapter we will assume your organization has a 20+ year perspective and that you do care and want to exist 20 years from now.

Visioning is an exercise where we envision what our business world will look like out into the future. We consider various business environment characteristics that may exist in the future. We consider what our competitive environment, our customer demand, and our resource availability will be like. And then we look at what will be required of our organization to get ready for this changed world. One of the authors worked with a Japanese company that looked 300 years into the future. They had a 300-year vision, a 100-year vision, a 50-year vision, a 20-year vision, and a 10-year vision. Some companies may see this as a little extreme, but this particular company is extremely successful and saw this level of visioning as critical in planning the company's future.

In scenario planning we consider what we learned in the visioning exercise, and we create various corporate scenarios for our organization. What will we do in the most adverse situation? How will our business change? What can we do to get ready for this change? Similarly, we look at the best conditions for our operating environment and ask a similar set of questions. How will we get ready for this positive environment? And thirdly, we perform this exercise again, this time focusing on the most likely scenario. What do we as a corporate team envision is the most realistic future state? And how do we get ready for this setting? In scenario planning, there is nothing magical about three scenarios. Some organizations feel the need to plan out a large number of scenarios. They want to be ready for every condition.

Visioning does not require scenario planning to be completed. However, effective scenario planning requires the completion of a visioning exercise. This will be better understood as we go through each of the two exercises. With this background we are now ready to discuss the visioning and scenario planning procedure in detail. Scenario planning is incorporated as part of the visioning process, but can be skipped if desired.

Visioning and Scenario Planning

An effective visioning exercise should provide an organization with a set of goals and objectives based on a look into the future. This is important because an effective strategy incorporates a long-term perspective and cannot be strictly focused on the problems that engage us here and now. Although current problems cannot be ignored, a long-term perspective may direct an organization's efforts away from short-term solutions and aim them toward an entirely different set of solutions.

A couple of excellent methodologies offer a long-term analysis of opportunities and help develop long-term solutions. These methodologies are detailed and are books all by themselves. For the reader that wants a deeper understanding of identifying long-term opportunities, these methodologies should be considered. However, for the purpose of this book, we will discuss a visioning methodology that offers more immediate results and drives us rapidly toward an executable strategic map.

The two in-depth problem-solving and visioning methodologies are

1. Breakthrough thinking
2. Concept management

Both are discussed in more detail in Appendix 9.1 and Appendix 9.2 at the end of this chapter.

In this chapter the focus will be on a visioning/scenario planning methodology that has been found to be effective for the majority of companies throughout the United States. As with all tools, it will need to be adapted and customized for your organization, but a generic look at the tool will be presented here.

This visioning exercise explores the long-range (10 to 40 years out) effects on the current operating environment. It involves the following steps, which will be discussed in more detail below:

1. Leadership orientation
2. An orientation briefing
3. A "homework" assignment for Visioning Exercise Workshop attendees
4. The workshop
5. Postworkshop wrap-up

Step 1: Leadership Orientation

We start most strategy programs with a leadership orientation that attempts to get leadership in sync with the process. We don't want leadership questioning the process when we are engaged in the strategic activity. Visioning is no exception and will also require a senior leadership briefing. During the leadership orientation we sit down with the CEO and the president of the company (the top three or four individuals in the leadership structure) and discuss the purpose, impact, and resource requirements of the workshop. We review what will happen during the workshop and how it will benefit the command. We ask what their expectations are for the workshop and how we can help meet those expectations. Typical expectations include the following:

- Perspective on the future work environment 5, 10, 20, and 40 years into the future. The timeline is set by the organization and can vary. Sometimes, at the corporate level, the timeline may be longer than the one used at the division level.
- Effects/impact this future environment will have on the organization
- Scenario planning—best case/worst case/most likely scenarios
- Plan for action—what changes does our organization need to consider as high-level priorities when developing a strategic plan
- Organizational unity and focus
- Dialogue on organizational change

Step 2: The Orientation Briefing

The orientation briefing is a 30-minute meeting with all future workshop attendees. The fourfold purpose of the meeting is to

1. Go through a series of seven slides (shown in the figures that follow) that explain the exercise (These are also the same slides that will be used during the exercise.)
2. Assign each of the attendees a homework assignment in preparation for the visioning exercise
3. Allow management to give direction and perspective
4. Answer any questions about the exercise

The following is an example of how the orientation briefing should proceed. The orientation brief is a presentation of the same set of slides that will be used during the workshop. However, during the orientation we will go through the slides in about 30 minutes, just to give everyone an overview of how the workshop will proceed. Slide 1 (Figure 9.1) shows the agenda for the workshop.

In this slide we explain that everyone will be given a homework assignment where they will be assigned a specific trend or driving force that they will be asked to research. They will need to bring their research findings on "environmental influences" to the workshop. In the workshop these findings will be

---

Agenda

Identify trends and driving forces
Sort trends and driving forces
Create an organizational vision
Develop alternative scenarios
    Worst case (for our business)
    Best case (for our business)
    Most likely case
Evaluate each scenario
    List the changes that will occur
    List the changes that will be required of our organization
Link the vision to the strategy
    Generate a vision statement
    Generate a mission statement
    Generate some "straw-men" organizational objectives

Figure 9.1 Slide 1: Agenda.

used for the brainstorming exercise that will start the vision-ing exercise.

Also, during this first slide we need to explain that the results of our brainstorming exercise will be analyzed and utilized to create a vision statement for your organization. From this we go to a scenario planning exercise. After the scenario planning, we are ready to generate organizational vision, mission, and some straw-man objectives that will be used in the SA&D (strategic alignment and deployment) exercise (in the next chapters).

The second slide (Figure 9.2) shows how environmental influences generate trends and driving forces and then their effects are categorized into one of the time frames that we will be analyzing. The time frames do not have to be the same as shown on the slide. There can be more or less, and the times can be different as well. It should be customized to meet the needs of your organization.

The third slide (Figure 9.3) prioritizes the impact of each of the identified trends and driving forces within each of the selected time frames.

The fourth slide (Figure 9.4) takes our prioritized trends and driving forces and utilizes them to develop scenarios in each of at least three cases:

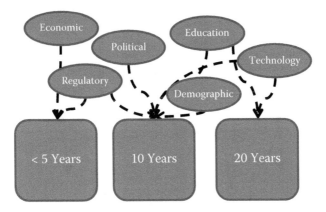

Figure 9.2 Slide 2: Trends and driving forces.

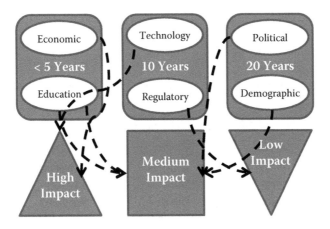

Figure 9.3 Slide 3: Impacts.

- Best case: If all the environmental influences work in our favor, what will the future look like for us?
- Worst case: If all the environmental influences work against us, what will the future look like for us?
- Most likely case: Given what we know today, what would be the most likely scenario for the future?
- Other cases can be generated if additional scenario options seem feasible.

The fifth slide (Figure 9.5) takes our trends and driving forces and maps them into a plan for action. It answers the

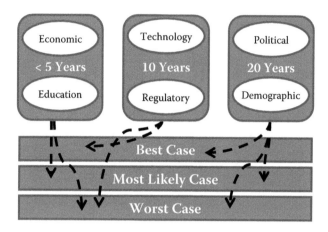

Figure 9.4 Slide 4: Scenario planning.

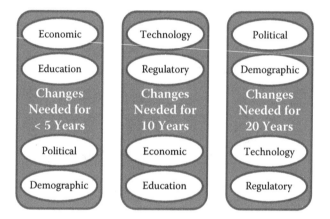

Figure 9.5 Slide 5: Plan for action.

questions "so what?" and "now what?" Here we explain how this data will be utilized to formalize an organizational strategic plan that takes the vision and mission and drives them down to goals, objectives, and tasks. It details out what the plan for action will look like.

The sixth slide (Figure 9.6) demonstrates that alignment is needed between the short-, medium-, and long-range changes and that the organization needs to look at this as a linear and focused process. Don't make changes in the short term that do not correlate with long-term trends.

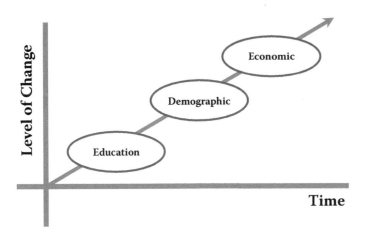

Figure 9.6 Slide 6: Change milestones.

Front-End Strategic Information			
Core Competencies:			
Vision:			
Mission:			
Defining the Customer:			
The Strategy Map			
Priorities and Goals:	Objectives / Strategies:	Metrics:	Tasks / Action Items:
Priority Statement: End State Statement:	Objective / Strategy Statement:	Metrics Statements:	Tasks / Action Item Statements:
Goal Statement:	Objective / Strategy Statement:	Metrics Statements:	Tasks / Action Item Statements:
	Objective / Strategy Statement:	Metrics Statements:	Tasks / Action Item Statements:

Figure 9.7 Slide 7: The strategy map.

Then, as a wrap-up, it is valuable to show one more slide (Figure 9.7), which is an example of what occurs after the completion of the visioning exercise. It shows the linkages between the Visioning Workshop and the SA&D strategy map. From here we take all our inputs from the current exercise and integrate them into the SA&D workshop. The results of the SA&D workshop give us a strategically aligned collection of tasks that are focused and then executed and will help us achieve our organizational goals.

Step 3: A "Homework" Assignment for Visioning Exercise Workshop Attendees

During the orientation meeting, a homework assignment will be given to each of the attendees to help them be more prepared for the actual workshop. The homework assignment sheet is self-explanatory and is the attached worksheet (Table 9.1).

Step 4: The Workshop

The workshop follows and uses the same slides that were reviewed in the orientation briefing (Step 3). The workshop is intended to be a very interactive discussion and is not a slide show. It is focused on the following:

1. An open review of each of the six "environmental impact" focus areas:
   a. Economics (inflation, trade alliances, trade embargos, international economics, etc.)
   b. Technology/energy
   c. Workplace demographics/staffing/HR (age, race, gender, education level, socioeconomic status, etc.)
   d. Regulation/politics (environmental, state and federal laws, etc.)
   e. International relations
   f. Security (physical security of our installations, property, people; cyberthreat, etc.)
   g. Strategic communications (to our members, stakeholders, the public, etc.)
   h. Growth (end strength, recruiting, retention, etc.)
   i. Capacity (our ability to perform, training, manning, etc.)
2. Each topic is addressed individually. Major "trends" are identified and posted on sticky notes on a board (Figure 9.1).

TABLE 9.1
**Trends and Driving Forces: Research Assignments
in Preparation for the Visioning Exercise**

Each member of the team will research two of the following areas, looking
for emerging trends and their causes. A show of hands will make sure that
the team sizes for each area have an approximately equal. During the
exercise, the team for each area will discuss their findings and solicit input
from the rest of the attendees.

We need to explore how trends in the following areas (select the areas that
are relevant—that have an effect on the performance of your organization)
will affect your organization over the next 5, 10, and 20 years.

1. Economics (inflation, trade alliances, trade embargos, international
   economics, etc.)
2. Technology
3. Energy
4. Workplace Demographics/Staffing/HR (age, race, gender, education
   level, socio-economic status...)
5. Regulation/Politics (environmental, state and federal laws...)
6. International Relations
7. Security (physical security of our installations/property/people, cyber
   threat...)
8. Strategic Communications (to our members, stakeholders, the public...)
9. Growth (end strength, recruiting, retention...)
10. Capacity (our ability to perform, training, manning...)
11. Natural Resources

New trends are constantly developing in these areas. What is happening to
them over the next decades? How will that affect your command? How will
those developments change what our organization looks like? How
successful will we be in the new environment? How comfortable or
uncomfortable will our future be? The environment is sure to change. We
need to research these areas so we can predict some of those changes and
plan for them.

Your assignment for the workshop is to bring to the discussion at least two
major future developments in each of the areas you are researching. (If you
are working in a group, bring two trends per person.)

Between now and the visioning workshop be mindful of what you hear
about your topic. Keep your antenna tuned to pick up little bits of
knowledge about what is happening in your assigned areas.

- Talk with people inside and outside of your organization, especially
  your customers and your suppliers.
- Notice what people are saying about it, what is being written about it.

Continued

TABLE 9.1 (continued)
Trends and Driving Forces: Research Assignments
in Preparation for the Visioning Exercise

- Ask people about it.
- Call people at other companies, at universities, or in the government and ask them what they are hearing.
- Read a couple of articles.
- Google it.
- Find a book on the topic.
- Cast a wide net and see what you learn.

We are looking to scan the environment and bring new and unique insights to the discussion—things we don't already know. We'll use those bits and pieces to figure out the major trends that are going to affect us in the future. This is not just "thought work." The quality of what you gather will literally determine the future course of your company.

3. After an environmental impact topic area has been thoroughly reviewed, the posted sticky notes are reviewed and reposted under a <5 year, 10 year, or 20+ year category (Figure 9.2). Then we move on to the next focus area (about 30 minutes to 1 hour per focus area).

4. After all the focus areas are reviewed, we should have a cluster of sticky notes in each of the time categories. The attendees are then asked to review these notes and put "dots" on those sticky notes that they consider to be high-priority trends (trends that will have a strong influence on the future performance of the command) (about 30 minutes as part of a break). See Figure 9.3. The items with the highest number of dots are the highest priority, the ones with no dots are the lowest priority, and those with only a few dots are medium priority.

5. In a group discussion, the high-priority trends are reviewed one at a time to determine what changes the company will need to consider as they prepare for this trend. These changes are recorded on sticky notes and posted on a new pad. Recurring changes are noted as higher priority than those that don't occur as often (about 1 hour).

6. *Optional exercise:* As an additional exercise, if time permits, it is valuable to do some scenario planning

(Figure 9.4). This requires looking at alternative future states. For example:

a. Best case: If all the environmental influences work in our favor, what will the future look like for us? What is the best possible set of circumstances from the perspective of our organization?

b. Worst case: If all the environmental influences work against us, what will the future look like for us? What is the worst possible set of circumstances from the perspective of our organization (consider each trend and the worst possible situation for that trend)?

c. Most likely case: Given what we know today, what would be the most likely scenario for the future?

d. Other cases can be generated if additional scenario options seem feasible.

Utilizing each of these alternative sets of circumstances, what is the scenario that our organization will find itself in? What scenario (plan of attack) should our organization consider for each of these sets of circumstances? What changes will our organization need to consider to be ready for these scenarios (about 3 to 4 hours, may need to occur on a second day)?

7. These "changes" will then be summarized and become part of the SWOT (strengths, weaknesses, opportunities, threats) in the SA&D exercise. Groups of these changes become critical priorities for the future of our organization (Figure 9.5). This should become your "plan for action."

Step 5: Postworkshop Wrap-up

After the workshop, all the trends and changes are summarized on a report. These will be used for future visioning exercises. A visioning/SA&D exercise should occur once a year. This data is also critical for initiating the SA&D strategy map exercise that is intended to be the next step after a visioning exercise. We'll discuss this in more detail in the next chapters.

Summary

At this point we have prepared ourselves for the development of a corporate strategy. In the next chapters we will take the visioning information that was generated in this chapter and use it as the foundation for creating the strategy map shown in Figure 9.7. Then, the last few chapters will show us how to take this map and drive it toward meaningful execution utilizing the Lean methodology and Lean tools.

Appendix 9.1: Breakthrough Thinking

Breakthrough thinking is a methodology that focuses on the tools needed for identifying creative solutions to both short-term and long-term problems. Numerous books are available that go into breakthrough thinking in great depth. The foundational books include the following:

1. Gerald Nadler and Shozo Hibino, *Breakthrough Thinking*, Rocklin, CA: Prima Publishing & Communications, 1990.
2. Gerald Nadler, Shozo Hibino, and John Farrell, *Creative Solution Finding*, Rocklin, CA: Prima Publishing & Communications, 1995.

Nadler and Hibino, the creators of the Breakthrough Thinking methodology, described a "paradigm shift in thinking" called "breakthrough thinking." Their methodology stressed that in order to solve difficult problems and analyze new opportunities in an attempt to find creative solutions, our present thinking paradigm must change. Gerald Nadler and Shozo Hibino published *Breakthrough Thinking* in 1990 and *Creative Solution Finding* in 1993. In these two books they defined a paradigm developed in Japan that caused a shift in thinking.

From a historical viewpoint, our thinking paradigms have been continuously shifting over time. Our conventional thinking paradigm (Descartes thinking) is out of date with a rapidly changing world and needs to shift to a newer thinking paradigm. In the 21st century, we have to be multi-thinkers who are able to use three thinking paradigms; God thinking, conventional (Descartes) thinking, and breakthrough thinking (BT).

For example, God thinking focuses on making decisions based on God's will. For some decisions, there is no need for analysis. Behavior is firmly dictated by God's will, our values systems, and our life philosophies. For example, moral or ethical issues are decided and are not open for discussion. Conventional thinking starts with an analysis process that focuses on fact or truth finding. When we make a decision, our behavior is based on the facts or on scientific truth. We need the facts to make our decisions. Breakthrough thinking starts with the ideal or ultimate objective. When we make a decision, we base our behavior on this objective.

The three thinking paradigms are completely different, and each has a different approach. We cannot neglect any of these three thinking paradigms because each has an influence in the decision-making process. We have to select and utilize each of these paradigms on a case-by-case basis. Someone who uses and interchanges these thinking paradigms is referred to as a multi-thinker.

Since there is no future that continues along the same lines as our past and present (because of the drastic changes going on in the world), we cannot find futuristic solutions based on past and present facts. Our thinking base should be changed away from facts and refocus on the substance, essence, or ideal.

To identify the substance of things is not easy. We have to transform ourselves from having a conventional machine view to a systems-oriented view. The traditional perspective of conventional thinking is to view things as a reductionistic machine, breaking everything down into elemental parts, and neglecting the "whole" organic view.

Breakthrough thinking suggests that *everything is a system*, which focuses BT on a holonic view. If we define everything as a system, then everything is a Chinese box, which means that a bigger box (system) includes a series of smaller boxes (systems). A small box (system) contains still smaller boxes (systems), and so on. Each box (system) has its purpose or purposes. If you repeatedly ask, What is the purpose? and then, What is the purpose of that purpose? and then, What is the purpose of that purpose of that purpose? and so on, you can reach the biggest box, which is *wholeness*. You can view everything from the perspective of this wholeness. BT calls this search the "purpose expansion."

BT consists of a thinking paradigm and thinking process. The thinking paradigm of BT is the opposite of the paradigm of conventional thinking. Its main points are expressed as seven principles:

1. Uniqueness principle: Always assume that the problem, opportunity, or issue is different. Don't copy a solution or use a technique from elsewhere just because the situation may appear to be similar. In using this principle, we have to think about the locus or solution space of the problem. This locus is defined using three points:
   a. Who are the major stakeholders? Who's viewpoint is most important?
   b. What is the location?
   c. When (what is the timing)?
2. Purposes principle: Explore and expand purposes to understand what really needs to be accomplished and to identify the substance of things. You can tackle any problem, opportunity, or issue by expanding purposes if you change your epistemology to a systems view. Understanding the context of purposes provides the following strategic advantages:
   a. Pursue the substance of things: We can identify the most essential focus purpose or the greater purpose, often referred to as the substance (core element) of things by expanding purposes.
   b. Work on the right problem or purpose: Focusing on right purposes helps strip away nonessential aspects to avoid working on just the visible problem or symptom.
   c. Improve the ability to redefine: Redefining is usually very difficult. Once you've redefined, you can have different viewpoints, each of which enables you to solve problems from different directions.

    d. Eliminate purpose/functions: From systems theory we learn that a bigger purpose may eliminate a smaller purpose. By focusing on the bigger purpose, you can eliminate unnecessary work, systems, or parts, which means that you can get more effective solutions.

    e. More options, more creative: If you have a purpose hierarchy, you have a lot of alternative solutions.

    f. Holonic view: Take a "big picture" perspective.

3. Solution-after-next (SAN) principle: Think and design futuristic solutions for the focus purpose and then work backward. Consider the solution you would recommended if in 3 years you had to start all over. Make changes today based on what might be the solution of the future. Learn from the futuristic ideal solution for the focus purpose and don't try learning from the past and present situations.

4. Systems principle: Everything we seek to create and restructure is a system. Think of solutions and ideas as a system. When you see everything as a system, you have to consider the eight elements of a system to identify the solution:

    a. Purpose: mission, aim, need

    b. Input: people, things, information

    c. Output: people, things, information

    d. Operating steps: process and conversion tasks

    e. Environment: physical and organizational

    f. Human enablers: people, responsibilities, skills, to help in the operating steps

    g. Physical enablers: equipment, facilities, materials to use in the operating steps

    h. Information enablers: knowledge, instructions

5. Needed information collection principle: Collect only the information that is necessary to continue the solution-finding process. Know your purposes for collecting data and information. Study the solutions, not the problems.

6. People design principle: Give everyone who will be affected by the solution or idea the opportunity to participate throughout the process of its development.

A solution will work only if people know about it and help to develop and improve it.
7. Betterment timeline principle: Install changes with built-in seeds of future change. Know when to fix it before it breaks. Know when to change it.

The BT process is an approach of reasoning toward a situation-specific solution using a design approach. It is an iterative, simultaneous process of mental responses based on the purpose–target–results approach (PTR approach). The three phases of PTR are as follows:

1. Purpose: Identifying the right solution by finding focus purposes, values, measures
2. Target: Targeting the solution of tomorrow—ideal SAN vision and target solution
3. Results: Getting and maintaining results toward implementation and systematization

For a more detailed discussion, please read the book noted above titled *Breakthrough Thinking*. It will offer you extensive detail on the BT process.

Appendix 9.2: Concept Management

Concept management is a methodology that focuses on the tools needed for reevaluating the way we look at and consider both short-term and long-term problems. Concept management incorporates all the principles of breakthrough thinking and integrates continuous process improvement (CPI) thinking. Numerous books are available that go into concept management in great depth. The foundational books include the following:

1. Gerhard Plenert and Shozo Hibino, *Making Innovation Happen: Concept Management through Integration*, Delray Beach, FL: St. Lucie Press, 1997.
2. Gerhard Plenert, *Reinventing Lean: Introducing Lean Management into the Supply Chain*, NY: Elsevier, 2007.

Breakthrough thinking and concept management are tools that developed sequentially. These tools can be utilized as a change model that focuses on (1) innovation and creativity, and (2) making sure we are "doing the right things." These tools focus on asking, Why are we doing this? and using the "purpose expansions" before asking, Are we doing this right? which tends to be the focus of the root cause analysis.

Concept management (CM) is a Japanese tool that integrates breakthrough thinking (BT), world class management (WCM), and total quality management (TQM). BT is the technique utilized to develop futuristic, leading-edge ideas. It moves away from the slowness and costliness of traditional root cause analysis commonly used in the United States and Europe. WCM offers the formal structure around which the ideas are turned into goals and a measurement–motivation system. TQM is the process for team-based idea/change implementation.

CM is an idea generation and implementation process used by companies like Toyota and Sony that breaks us out of the traditional, analytical thinking common to companies such as the Ford Motor Company, which uses the TOPS program, or the Russian TRIZ program. Instead, CM focuses on forming a purpose hierarchy through a series of steps.

Concept management uses the terms *concept* to mean innovative purpose-driven change creation and *management* to focus on organization and leadership. Therefore concept management is innovative, change-oriented, purpose-driven (goal-focused), creative leadership. This leadership occurs through the integration of ideas, primarily the ideas expressed in two leading-edge philosophies: BT and WCM.

As seen in Appendix 9.1, Nadler and Hibino defined a "paradigm shift in thinking" called "breakthrough thinking." Thinking paradigms have shifted over history, for example, primitive, early Greek, classical Greek, God thinking, Descartes, and others. From the historical viewpoints, our thinking paradigms have been continuously shifting over time. Our conventional thinking paradigm (Descartes thinking) is out of date with a rapidly changing world and needs to shift again to a new thinking paradigm, BT. In the 21st century, we have to be multi-thinkers who are able to simultaneously use all three thinking paradigms: God thinking, conventional (Descartes) thinking, and breakthrough thinking.

WCM is broad in its application, and numerous publications discuss the subject in detail (see Plenert's book *eManager* or his book *Making Innovation Happen: Concept Management through Integration*). However, to get a clear understanding of how world class managers manage change, the focus would be on

1. People: Employees and stakeholders are the source of change opportunities. They need to be motivated properly through an appropriate measurement system to drive change.
2. Customers: Customers are the reason for change. To be competitive we need to give our customers a clear reason why they should not buy from anyone else but us.
3. Performance: Performance requires focus on a goal, whether it is financial or quality or some other focus. Then we need to measure, monitor, and offer feedback information about our performance.
4. Competitors: Competition creates fear, but it also creates opportunity. Competitors need to be analyzed and understood in order to be defeated.
5. Future: The future is coming, whether we're ready for it or not. If we're not ready for it, it will pass us by, along with our customers and competitors.
6. Integration: Through integration everyone and everything work together. Managers are not merely bosses; they are leaders and facilitators by example. They work side by side with the employee.

WCM is not a system or a procedure; it is a culture. It is a continually molding process of change and improvement. It is a competitive strategy for success.

In the United States, TQM has fallen into disfavor because of its analytical approach to change. The analysis process is deemed too slow to be competitive. But that is primarily because TQM utilized root cause analysis. With breakthrough thinking we can revisit and reinvigorate our use of TQM.

There are two major aspects to TQM: one philosophical, and the other operational. From the philosophical we get guidelines and from the operational we get techniques. Traditionally, the philosophy of TQM could be stated as, "Make sure you're doing the right things before you worry about doing things right." TQM focuses on careful, thoughtful analysis. However, the analysis should be creative, innovative, and "innoveering" oriented. It wants to make sure that we are implementing positive, goal-focused changes before we move a muscle.

TQM is an enterprise-wide change model. Some people define TQM as making the entire organization responsible for product or service quality. To some TQM is a behavior-based philosophy of motivation and measurement. TQM does, in fact, require a cultural shift for all members of an organization in that it uses an entire philosophy about how businesses should be run. TQM is filled with ideas and attitudes:

Attitude of desiring and searching out change
Think culture—move from copying to innovating
Focus on the goal
Measurement–motivation planning
Top-to-bottom corporate strategy
Company-wide involvement
Clear definition and implementation of quality
Education, training, and cross-training
Integration and coordination
Small, step-by-step improvements

TQM implementation starts with a coordinating team, often referred to as a Quality Council. This is a team composed of high-level corporate leaders from all the functional areas, usually at the vice president level. This team is appointed by the CEO and operates under the CEO's direction. The CEO actively directs the endeavors of the team and is often an active team member. This Quality Council is then responsible for organizing, chartering, and measuring the performance of the other TQM teams within the organization. It oversees the installation, training, performance, and measurement of the other teams. This team aims to keep all teams focused on the corporate goal and vision.

Using these Japanese methodologies—TQM, BT, and WCM—concept management works in a series of stages:

1. Concept creation: The development and creation of new ideas through the use of BT and its innovative methods of creativity.
2. Concept focus: The development of a target that includes keeping your organization focused on core values and a core competency. Then, utilizing the creativity generated by concept creation, a set of targets is established using WCM and a road map is developed to help to achieve the targets.
3. Concept engineering: This is the engineering of the ideas, converting the fuzzy concepts into usable, consumer-oriented ideas. TQM, through the use of a focused, chartered team and through a managed SPS process, helps to manage the concept from idea to product.
4. Concept in: This is the process of creating a market for the new concept. The concept is transformed into a product, service, or system using WCM techniques. BT may be used to help develop a meaningful and effective market strategy.
5. Concept management: Both the management of the new concepts as well as a change in the management approach (management style) are affected by the new concept. Concept management is the integration of the first four stages of the concept management process (creation, focus, engineering, and in).

For more detail on the concept management process, please read the book noted above *Making Innovation Happen: Concept Management through Integration*.

10

Vision/Mission/
Customer
Identification/
Priorities/
End State/Goals

**Driving
Strategy
to Execution**

Organizational
Framework

1 –Trends
2 –Role
3 –Options
4 –Process

World Class
Status

15 –Defining WC
16 –Conclusions

5 –Culture
6 –Alignment
7 –Metrics
8 –Integration

9 –Visioning
10 –Vision / Mission
11 –Priorities
12 –Governance
13 –Lean
14 –Repeat

Organizational
Performance

Strategy
Execution

Well, if there's no time for fun, doc, then what are we trying to save the planet for?

—Major West
Lost in Space

This chapter will start building the strategy map. The strategy-building exercise is usually accomplished over a 3 to 5 day period in an off-site location to avoid distractions. The team is locked in, similar to the visioning exercise in the last chapter, and they give their full attention to creating an effective and useful strategy for the organization. The next few chapters will each discuss the components of the strategy map, how it should be constructed, and what it means.

As we work our way through this chapter, we will discuss all the initial high-level elements of an executable strategy map. We will focus on the following:

- Core competencies
- The vision statement
- The mission statement
- The customer
- The corporate priorities
- The end state for each priority
- The goals for each priority

We will start by getting philosophical about goals and goal setting with the statement "A journey of 1000 miles begins with a single step." Goals give purpose and direction to what we are doing. We need to focus on a clearly defined target to get direction in what we are trying to accomplish. In the development of corporate goals we have the following stages:

- Defining the core competencies
- The vision
- The mission
- The strategy
- The priorities for your operation

Core Competencies

The first step, defining core competencies, is not really a goal as much as it is an introspective look at what you're good at. Are you good at all things, like sourcing, manufacturing, distribution, retailing, and customer service? Probably not. So which one(s) is your organization really good at, the rest being the necessary evils that you need to tolerate and optimize as part of your business? The core competency is the combination of individual technologies and production skills that underlie a company's productive processes.

In defining the core competency, we are attempting to identify what we are better at than anyone else. What is it that makes us unique? What is our competitive advantage? What should we exploit for strategic success? Two tools are helpful in the development and definition of the core competency. These tools can also be used in later steps of the goal setting process.

The two tools are the SWOT (strengths, weaknesses, opportunities, and threats) analysis and the competitive position analysis. In the SWOT analysis we utilize a cross-functional team of individuals in a brain-storming environment to search out the *strengths* of the company, its *weaknesses* and shortcomings that later become opportunities for improvements, the *opportunities* of the organization, and last of all the *threats* to the success of the company. These are the four SWOT elements, and after the SWOT analysis you would have generated a long list of ideas for strategic development.

The competitive position analysis focuses on the competitive environment under which you operate. It involves taking a look at who your competitors are and what their strengths and weaknesses are. It also focuses on the demands of the marketplace, looking for areas that have not been serviced and that may offer strategic advantages.

Following are some examples of core competencies (sometimes referred to as capabilities) of certain companies:

- Sony—miniaturization
- Canon—optics, imaging, and microprocessor controls
- Honda—engines and power trains

After defining the core competency (what a company is really good at), we then break the core competency down even more. For example, are you good at distributing everywhere, just in the United States, or just in the Pacific Northwest? By going through this process of identification you end up with a clear definition of what your core competencies are. After you know what you're good at, capitalize on it and use it in conjunction with your visioning information (from the last chapter) to build a plan for your organization's growth and future. This identification step gives you a basis for the development of your vision, mission, and strategy.

The Vision Statement

Where there is no vision, the people perish.

—Proverbs 29:18

To become a visionary company you need two things:

1. a guiding philosophy and value system—a vision
2. a challenging short-term mission that quantifies the vision

In each stage of the goal development process we drill down to more detail than the level we were at before it. For example, the vision is one or two sentences stating where the enterprise is going. It is the sense of purpose of an enterprise, its reason for being, and its guiding philosophy. A vision statement builds unity throughout the organization. Utilize the information from the last chapter to generate a consensus-based vision. It doesn't have to be long, but it has to give the organization purpose.

The vision statement is a short phrase that expresses the long-term objectives of an organization, keeping in mind the values and core competencies of the organization. The vision should provide employees with a clear image that they can identify with. Some excellent examples are as follows:

> To make a contribution to the world by making tools for the mind that advance humankind
>
> **—Steve Jobs**
> *Apple Computer*

> To make people happy
>
> **—Walt Disney**

The Mission Statement

Unlike the vague, undefined, timeless vision statement, the mission statement is a series of defined goals for the enterprise that are aimed at the vision. The mission has a definite, measurable goal and should be date-stamped with a finish line. The mission should be challenging (see the "Goal Characteristics" section later in this chapter). One of the best examples of an excellent mission is

> achieving the goal, before this decade is out, of landing a man on the moon and returning him safely to earth.
>
> **—President John F. Kennedy, 1962**

Defining the Customer

As interesting as it may seem, most organizations don't agree who their customer really is. Various levels of the organization will give different answers to the question "Who is our customer?" Sometimes the answer goes directly to the customer list of the organization. And sometimes we find ourselves tangled into discussion about the employee, or their families, or society being the ultimate customers. Are we in business to thrill our customers, or to stay in business, or to offer stability for our employees? A discussion that defines the customer will become a vital part of the strategy development process because we usually have a strategic priority that is something like *Increase customer satisfaction.*

The Change Process

Marriage should war incessantly with that monster that is the ruin
of everything. This is the monster of habit.

—Honore De Balzac
French writer

Now we are ready to take a quick look at the change process to
see how it ties into the goals and strategies we establish. Our
vision and mission should have focused on change (improvement). We will implement this change through a series of strategic steps. There are two sources of change:

1. the changes you invoke yourself and
2. the changes that are happening to you.

This chapter has focused on the changes that you invoke yourself. However, there are still those changes that happen to you
that require contingency plans. You can't expect everything to
roll along perfectly. Life is filled with surprises. The better you
are prepared to roll with the punches and the better you are
prepared with contingency plans, the more likely you will be
able to achieve your eventual enterprise goals.

But goals aren't just for the enterprise. Goals should also be
a part of your life and your family's life. What do you want to be
when you grow up? What do you want to have accomplished in
10 years? in 20 years? How about the goals of your family? World
class requires being world class in the home as well as on the job.

World class change managers need targets to measure
world class performance. In this chapter we have discussed
core competencies, vision statements, and mission statements. Next we will go on to identify the strategic areas we
need to have quantifiable goals in that in turn will focus
back on the vision and mission of the enterprise.

The Strategy

Without developing and understanding the strategy, even
the simplest goal is impossible to achieve. The problem with

strategy is there are about a million different strategy models. I will focus primarily on those strategic areas that are the most critical to helping you become a world class manager.

World class strategies focus on world class competitiveness. Some of the competitive trends for the next decade include

- rapid change in technology and markets
- more global competitors
- environmental consciousness
- decentralization and globalization
- shrinking company sizes (strategic alliances)
- closer links to customers and suppliers
- a competitive emphasis on cost reduction and a customer-oriented quality improvement, and a stronger priority on flexibility and time-to-market responsiveness
- borderless companies
- removal of departmentalization

Some of the key principles of world class competitiveness include

- focus on the people (primary employees)
- focus on the customer
- a quality and productivity stance
- a global perspective
- time-based competition
- a technological orientation
- information management
- an integrative stance
- focused measurement
- a value-added decision approach
- continuous training and education

These trends and principles need to be integrated into a strategic plan for the organization. So what is a strategy? Figure 10.1 diagrams the format of a corporate strategy that we will be using in this book. It's not necessarily the best, and it's definitely not the only format that's available, but it is one that has been successfully utilized.

Front-End Strategic Information			
Core Competencies:			
Vision:			
Mission:			
Defining the Customer:			
The Strategy Map			
Priorities and Goals:	Objectives / Strategies:	Metrics:	Tasks / Action Items:
Priority Statement: End State Statement: Goal Statement:	Objective / Strategy Statement:	Metrics Statements:	Tasks / Action Item Statements:
	Objective / Strategy Statement:	Metrics Statements:	Tasks / Action Item Statements:
	Objective / Strategy Statement:	Metrics Statements:	Tasks / Action Item Statements:

Figure 10.1 The strategy map.

The strategy, like the mission and vision statement, should focus on the core competencies of the business unit or corporation. The strategy specifies the scope and boundaries of the business unit. It identifies the basis for achieving and maintaining competitive advantage. It describes how the resources of the business unit will be utilized to achieve the focused corporate mission. It determines the competitive priorities of the business unit, which include

- cost competitiveness—for example, K-Mart versus Sears, unit costs and delivery costs
- time competitiveness—FedEx versus the U.S. postal system, responsiveness and time to market
- quality competitiveness—K-Mart versus Sears, generics versus brand name products, performance and conformance
- dependability—fax versus telegram, the reliability of delivery commitments and service level and responsiveness

- flexibility—Taiwanese businesses versus the U.S. government, adaptability to change and customized products or services
- technology—ability to innovate, new product introduction, tinkering rather than changing, and speed and timing of change implementation

Although these competitive priorities are recognized and accepted as crucial elements in the development of an effective strategy, rarely do they become a part of the measurement–motivation system for the management of an enterprise. This is another example of verbalizing a goal without putting any power behind it. The strategy is only as valuable as the power and commitment that is placed behind it.

> Lord, I confess that I am not what I ought to be, but I thank you, Lord, that I'm not what I used to be.
>
> **—Maxie Dunnan**

Now that we have determined what the characteristics of a competitive business strategy entail and what its competitive priorities should focus on, we are ready to look at some of the strategy models that exist. These models contain areas of consideration that an ideal world class business strategy should consider.

> ...long-range thinking is as rare in the boardroom as in the White House...
> ...business is as confused as are the politicians...
> ...we are moving from a brute force to a brain force economy...
> ...knowledge is the new capital replacing stock or land holdings...
>
> **—Alvin Toffler**

Strategy Models

I recently heard the saying that behind every good man is a surprised mother-in-law. Similarly, behind every effective corporate strategy is a surprised manager. There are numerous models for strategic competitiveness. Each of these models gives us a slightly different insight into what our competitive strategies should be. Again, there is no correct answer. However, as we develop our priorities and goals, these different models may offer the reader some insights for the development of their own strategic plans.

Each of these models focuses on corporate excellence through world class management strategies. These models are all valuable in helping develop a strategic plan that details out our strategic process. For example, the Hall and Nakane model[*] breaks competitiveness into four quadrants, each of which requires strategic attention, possibly in the form of a priority:

1. *External technical factors*—the external and worldwide environment factors, such as government policies (fiscal and monetary policy, the taxation system, trade policies, industrial development policies, and social and ecological regulatory policies)
2. *Internal technical factors*—internal (within country) factors, such as technical capability, access to capital, technical advance for product design, process design, and computer information systems
3. *Cultures, philosophy, and customs (external)*—external and worldwide environment factors relating to the socioeconomic environment (race, languages and cultures, religions and values, the work ethic, educational systems and values, the health of people, economic and legal systems, support for technical advance, and the concept of companies and management)
4. *Cultures, philosophy, and customs (internal)*—internal (within country) factors relating to management philosophies, such as concept and culture of the company, organization structure, human resources management, attitude toward change, competitive strategy, targeting of markets, and the method of manufacturing improvement.

This model highlights a focus on global strategy. It also introduces the idea of a company culture, which contains the

[*] Robert W. Hall and Jinichiro Nakane, "Developing Flexibility for Excellence in Manufacturing: Summary Results of a Japanese-American Study," *Target* (Summer 1998) vol. 4, no. 2, p. 18.

philosophy, values, aspirations, and beliefs that the company has about itself and its people. This can differentiate it from other firms in the industry.

Another effective model for world class management strategies, demonstrated by Burnham,[*] breaks strategic planning into two areas:

1. *External factors*—competition, economic conditions, technology level, change in technology, government regulation, substitutions, and the product life cycle
2. *Internal factors*—market share, profitability, resources, logistics management, and manufacturing

A third model can be pulled from the publications of Adler, McDonald, and McDonald.[†] It would suggest focusing on the following strategic areas:

- strategic policies—personnel (recruitment, development, evaluation, and rewards), technical projects (selection, termination, and project management), quality assurance, intellectual properties, funding, facilities and equipment, structure (functional organization and authority), interfunctional linkages, external linkages, and regulatory compliance
- adjustment processes—strength, weaknesses, opportunities, and threats

A fourth model for corporate strategy could be[‡]:

- customer and markets
- technology and its characteristics
- performance review systems

[*] John B. Burnham, "Systematic Improvements in Physical Distribution or 'Why Can't We Just Do It Like We Used To?'" *APICS 34th Conference Proceedings* (Falls Church, Virginia: APICS) 1991, pp. 305–310.
[†] You can find out more about this model from Paul S. Adler, William D. McDonald, and Fred McDonald, "Strategic Management of Technical Functions," *Sloan Management Review* (Winter 1992) pp. 19–37.
[‡] See Timothy M. Mojonnier, "Top Management's Role in Fostering and Managing Positive Organizational Change," *APICS 37th Conference Proceedings* (Falls Church, VA: APICS) 1994, pp. 49–51.

- compensation systems
- organizational structure
- competition
- personnel policies
- financial position
- macro- and microeconomic variables
- information systems

A fifth model for the development of a corporate strategy focuses on capitalizing on the competitive advantage (core competency) of an enterprise. Michael Porter's model[*] discusses the strategy of diversification and how each business unit needs to define its roles (strategies) and to fit them into the corporate strategy.

> Corporate strategy is what makes the corporate whole add up to more than the sum of its business unit parts.
>
> **—Michael E. Porter**

A model for a world class corporate or business unit's strategic planning that the author has successfully used in the past would emphasize a focus on the following strategic areas:

- people—employees (education and training, empowerment, teamwork, organizational structure, and staff functions), customers (involvement), and vendors (integration)
- integration—information and the elimination of barriers
- globalization
- measurement—internal performance (quality, productivity, and efficiency), external performance (added value to society, customer-perceived quality, market share), internal factors (capacity, equipment, and operational performance), external factors (competition, economic conditions, and government regulations), focus, and motivation

---

[*] For more information on competitive strategy, see the following publications from Michael Porter: *Competitive Strategy* (Free Press, 1980); *Competitive Advantage* (Free Press, 1985); "From Competitive Advantage to Corporate Strategy," *Harvard Business Review* (May–June 1987) pp. 43–59.

- continuous change process focused on adding value—elimination of waste; identifying strengths, weaknesses, opportunities, and threats
- time-based competition—time-to-market strategy
- technology—funding, facilities, and equipment

Let's look at each of these strategic areas in more detail.

People. You need a strategy that identifies, incorporates, and empowers people, especially the employees of the business unit. Next, you need a strategy that relates to customers. Customer satisfaction is the second most important principle to success. Next comes the suppliers. Their involvement and integration will help them make better products for you and will give you valuable insights into how to make your product better.

Integration. You need to drop the internal and external barriers. These include job titles, departments, and information barriers. Integration needs to exist physically (mix the different staff functions together in the same room), informationally (don't have separate databases for different departments as the information also needs to flow easily from top to bottom and from bottom to top), and in the processes (your output, information, or product, whatever it is you produce, needs to be passed from area to area, not thrown "over the wall" to each other organizationally; keep the employee designations and titles vague and treat everyone as an equal). Chapter 12 focuses heavily on the integration issues.

Globalization. We are part of a big world that is affected by international transactions. We need to be aware of how they affect us.

Measurement. Defining a measurement–motivational system is at the root of developing a strategic plan. We need to be able to demonstrate, over a defined period of time, that we are able to do our part in achieving the mission of the organization.

Continuous change process focused on adding value. We need to add value to ourselves, our organization, and society as a whole. Our strategic plan should motivate us toward adding value, which also includes the identification and elimination of waste.

Time-based competition. Time, like change, can be our enemy or our friend. Presently, for most U.S. firms, time is an enemy because our time-to-market performance is so poor. We are enormously effective at developing technology, but we are lousy at implementing it. For example, who developed the air bag? The United States. Who was first in installing it into their cars? Japan and Europe.

Technology. Technology is often the most effective tool for positive change. We need to develop a strategy that defines us as an organization and focuses on long-term technological improvements, as opposed to short-term "patch-it-up and keep-it-running" technologies.

Whatever strategy model you desire to follow, the following rules apply:

1. No one in the organization should be left without a goal (strategy). Everyone, from janitor to CEO, should have a goal. For example, Walt Disney Company orients everyone into the big corporate picture and teaches them how they fit in, even if they are only a temporary, 6-week employee.
2. Strategies should have short-term (less than 1 year), mid-term (1 to 5 years) and long-term (more than 10 years) targets. Each of the strategic areas needs a 1-year and a 20-year target to focus on.
3. The best strategy model to fit your enterprise does not yet exist. You'll have to develop it yourself. You can use the ideas from these example models, but you need to develop your own model.
4. Contingencies need to be established. A strategy is only as good as external influences (changes) allow it to function. Contingent strategies are strategies that help us plan for external changes without giving up the focus on our goals. A contingency is an alternative route to get to our destination. The more thought that is put into our contingency strategies (the more we plan for potential problems), the more likely that goal achievement will occur.

A philosopher was asked, "What do you do when you reach a fork in the road?" He answered very simply, "Take it."

Now it's time to combine what we've learned about the strategy. The strategy should

- Be developed at multiple levels—corporate strategy and business unit strategy
- Focus on the mission statement or higher-level business strategy
- Identify areas of competitiveness within each of the functional strategic areas of your selected strategic model
- Focus on the competitive trends and priorities
- Integrate the key competitive principles for strategy
- Contain quantifiable, time-stamped goals

At this point you should have a good feel for the types of areas and goals that your strategy should include. These will help define your priorities, end states, and goals.

Developing the Strategy: Priorities

Looking at Figure 10.1 we see the front-end strategic information filled in at the top of the form. Each of these inputs will probably take about 1 hour of teamwork. With these completed we are ready to work on the strategy map, which is the bottom half of the form. The area listed shows the breakdown of only one of the priorities. Normally, an organization will have three to five priorities, so the strategy map will be several pages long.

An organization's priorities were identified during the visioning exercise. The highest three to five priorities should have been identified, and these will become the priorities listed in the strategy map. The priority is further refined by describing the end state and the goal for each priority. Before we describe each of these elements of the priority in depth, we should delve further into some of the philosophy behind goal setting.

The reason for goal development is to identify and quantify goals for each strategic priority and focus on bringing that priority area in focus with the mission of the enterprise. The process of establishing priorities and their related goals takes a class syllabus approach to business. Imagine if in college, when you take a class, the professor comes to you and says, "Keep doing what you're doing; you're doing great, and at the end of the semester I'll evaluate you." As the semester goes along, the professor continues with his vague, directionless information. Then, when the end of the year rolls around, the professor says, "Well, you all did OK, so I'll pass some of you and flunk some of you," never indicating why some were passed and some were flunked. If this were true, the students would be screaming and demanding details of what is expected of them. Unfortunately this directionless methodology seems to be an acceptable way to run a business. Rather, in college, when you take a class, the professor gives you a class syllabus. This defines the course requirements, what needs to be accomplished for successful completion of the course, and the timing of the course. Using the class syllabus approach would give everyone in the organization clear objectives and not leave them blindfolded. Everyone knows what they're shooting at.

An additional problem for an empowered organization is that leadership is challenged with making sure each and every employee is involved in goal setting. This is critical if leadership wants buy-in and ownership of the priorities and goals that get established. If the employees have buy-in, then they'll make it successful.

To discuss goals effectively, we need to discuss the types of goals that exist and their characteristics. First we will focus on the types of goals. Later we will have a section focused on the characteristics of good goals. It is also possible to have secondary goals, but they need to complement, not to draw away from, the primary goal.

The priorities and goals of an enterprise set the value system of the organization. We in the United States have grown accustomed to the idea that there is only one correct goal for a business enterprise, and that is to have a financial focus. Interestingly, this goal is in the minority when taking an international perspective. Businesses around the world have four major groupings of goals:

financial,
operational,
employee based, and
customer based.

Each of these groupings has specific characteristics. For example, I have listed the goals in order, from short-term orientation to long-term orientation. Let's discuss each of these goal types specifically.

Financial goals include goals such as

- increase profits
- decrease costs
- increase sales
- increase return on investment
- increase return on net assets
- financial ratios

Financial goals are very short sighted and tend to be oriented toward quarterly or annual results. The short-sightedness of these goals stems a lot from the lack of trust that we have for each other. For example, stockholders don't trust the board of directors, the board does not trust the CEO, the CEO does not trust the vice presidents, who don't trust middle management, and so on. The result is that each level monitors the level below it on short-term financial measures.

If, for example, the CEO wants to introduce massive technological changes that will take several years to show a return, then he or she will be out of a job after the first or second year of losses. The CEO will have difficulty convincing the board that the benefits of the change are just around the corner. That's exactly what happened to Florida Power and Light. Florida Power and Light implemented a total quality improvement—a continuous change and improvement program called the quality improvement program (QIP). The benefits from the improvements were so dramatic that they were the first non-Japanese company to win the Deming Award, which is Japan's most prestigious national quality award. However, the implementation of this improvement program had extensive front-end costs, and the result was that after about 3 years of losses, the board became impatient and untrusting of the CEO. The board threw out the CEO along with his participative management style and all his continuous improvement ideas and installed an authoritarian CEO that keeps everything secret. Suddenly, employees who were formerly involved in the organization and its changes now have no idea from one day to the next what's going on within the organization.

Short-term financial measures ruled the day at Florida Power and Light, as they do in most United States organizations. But, in spite of the short-sighted negatives, financial goals can, and often are, used to affect positive growth and change. The key to success seems to be in the realization that long-term visions and missions are not achieved when they are restricted by short-term measures that don't focus on the long-term goals.

Operational goals have caught on in some parts of Europe. Operational goals tend to be more long term than financial goals. Additionally, achieving operational goals tends to have, as a by-product, the achievement of financial objectives. Operational goals would include, for example, the following:

- improved quality
- improved productivity
- reduced inventory
- increased throughput
- reduced scrap
- improved customer service level

It is easy to see how achieving each of these goals would improve profits. Additionally, these goals tend to be nonconflicting (see the discussion and example of conflicting financial goals in the "Goal Characteristics" section of this chapter). These goals tend to be long term because success tends to be measured incrementally. For example, a relatively small 10 percent inventory reduction each year for 10 years would lead to an enormous (65 percent cumulative) inventory reduction after 10 years, which, of course, would supply us with a similar increase in profitability.

Employee-based goals like employee permanence and stability are important goals that are used quite often in Japan. The primary reason for the popularity of these goals is that they support a participative relationship with the employees, rather than an authoritarian one. But there is a lot of misunderstanding about what this means and doesn't mean. For example, it doesn't mean that a company should ignore profitability any more than a successful, profit-oriented company can ignore its employees. It simply means that successful, happy employees create a successful, happy company. Let me explain, through a series of steps, how this goal works.

1. The goal of the company is to give its employees permanence and a steady growth path.
2. To accomplish this you need to be in business longer than any competitor that is building your product.
3. This is achieved by being successful at your product, more successful than any competitor.
4. Product successfulness is measured in terms of market share control.
5. Market share control is captured by whatever means.
6. When market share control is achieved, you have control of the product pricing, and therefore can recover any losses incurred while attempting to gain market share, hence profitability.

Note that the key goal, the one that started this entire series of events, is employee satisfaction.

FedEx, from its inception, has put its people first both because it is right to do so and because it is good business as well.

> Our corporate philosophy is succinctly stated: People-Service-Profit (P-S-P).
>
> **—Frederick W. Smith**
> *Chairman and CEO, FedEx*

A *customer-based goal* often gets confused with a quality-based goal. Quality is a strategy for achieving any of the goals. But quality itself is not a goal because it is defined and interpreted in so many different ways. For example, in the United States most companies who claim they have a quality product in fact have satisfied only some internal measure of quality. For most factories, a quality product is defined as one that meets engineering specifications—it has absolutely nothing to do with the customer.

The international measure for quality, the International Organization for Standardization (ISO) 9000 certification process, supports this "internal quality" perspective (see Chapter 12 for a more detailed discussion). In Europe, where the ISO 9000 process originated, there is the claim that Germany's quality is higher. But, unfortunately, this means only that their engineering standards are higher, not that the product is more customer oriented. Therefore, I can be "quality" and still not have satisfied a single customer.

World class quality lies in customer satisfaction, not engineer satisfaction. A world class quality product would be one about which

> the customer is so excited that they wouldn't think of going anywhere else to get it!

How do you know if you are customer-goal oriented? If you were, you would spend time with your customer at your customer's location, and your customer would spend time with you and your employees at your location. You would share, discuss, interact, learn, and create ideas (innovate) together. The customer would be an integral part of your planning circle. The reason for all this interaction is that you cannot satisfy a customer if you don't understand what they need or want.

I have listed the targets from shortest term to longest term, from easiest to implement to hardest, and from most objective to most subjective. Let's take a look at the differences between these goals.

Financial and operational goals are easy to measure. It's all in the data and can be displayed neatly on a graph. Working with employees and customers is vague and not quite as quantifiable. Maybe that's why we shy away from them. However, companies like FedEx and Toyota have found a very definite way to quantify their performance. It just takes a little more effort. But is it worth it? All the Baldrige and Deming award winners seem to think so. They all fall into one of these last two categories.

What we have achieved, at this point, is the need to establish a goal. This goal takes the form of a vision and mission statement, and later we set goals for each priority. There are two ways to come up with both of these statements:

bottom up and top down

The top-down approach would be to have the CEO, in conjunction with the vice presidents, develop the vision statement. Then, the mission statement is developed out of the vision generated by the top. The bottom-up approach would be to have middle or lower management define what they see the mission of the organization as being and then define a vision out of this synergistic mission. This helps adapt the organization to its own capabilities, since what works well in one business rarely works perfectly in another.

The bottom-up approach has demonstrated ownership and commitment by the employees toward the goals and has therefore become very popular with companies that are employee or customer based in their goal structure. No matter how the vision and mission statements are developed, the purpose of both documents is to develop a series of back-to-back targets that we can shoot at. These statements need to fit the employees. They need to be realistic, and they need to be communicated.

Often, we find that the employees, when given a say in the goal-setting process, are tougher on themselves than upper management would have been.

If you fail to plan, you plan to fail.

Goal Characteristics

If we were to pick the ideal target, what would it look like? It would be easy to see, focused (precise enough so that he knows exactly what he's shooting for), well defined, and custom designed to challenge his abilities. So why am I making such a big deal out of setting a goal? Because the typical business plan of a company reads like a wish list of all good things and is totally worthless. Having lots of business goals is as useful as not having any if they are not focused on a common vision. The goals soon get in each other's way. Goal setting should not be a process of setting high goals to drive employees to unrealistic ends. Nor should goal attainment result in a compromise of easy-to-attain steps. A good target should be realistic and attainable.

Specifically, all goals should have several characteristics (most goals do not have all of these characteristics, but you should try to include as many as possible):

- participatively created by and matched to the employees
- shared
- nonconflicting
- able to allow for and encourage change
- simple but not simplistic
- precise
- measurable
- uncompromised
- focused
- achievable yet challenging

Let's consider these characteristics in more detail.

Participatively created by and matched to the employees. Employees that participate in the goal development process maintain an ownership in the goals and feel personally challenged to achieve those goals. The goals are no longer "company" goals; rather they are "my" goals. This is what was meant when we discussed the employees developing the mission statement and then consolidating this into a vision. This is broader than the old concept of management by objectives (MBO), where the employees sit down with their supervisor and set goals for themselves. Participative goal setting is where the employees establish corporate goals, and not just individual goals.

Shared. One of the biggest "sins" of goal making is to not communicate the goal to the individuals that are responsible for achieving the goals. I have lost count of the number of companies who have said to me, "We don't show our employees our business plan because it is confidential," meaning that only strategic management employees are allowed to look at them. My question is, "How can you expect the employees to hit a target they cannot see?" No one can do that. Employees need to know what the goal is, how it is going to be measured, whether or not you are making progress toward the goal, and they should receive part of (share in) the reward of achieving the goal.

> A hidden goal is as useful as no goal, for no one will know if you succeeded.

Nonconflicting. Financial goals are often conflicting, but nonfinancial goals can be as well. Let's consider a recent financial example. The financial goals of this organization were to increase profits, increase sales, decrease costs, and increase the return on net assets. On the surface, this seems like a reasonable set of goals. However, under closer examination we see that these goals are conflicting and therefore impossible to achieve simultaneously. The result is something similar to what we see in Figure 10.2. For about the first 90 percent of the month we have steady output, working toward minimizing cost and maximizing profit. This is because we are working efficiently. Then, during the last 10 percent of the month we put on a rush trying to push as much product out the door as possible. We have thrown efficiency, profit, and cost reduction

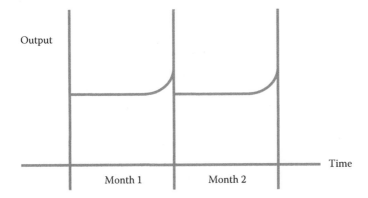

Figure 10.2 Conflicting goals.

to the wind. We send people scurrying around in an attempt to get employees to work in smaller batch sizes so that we can get a few extra product units (orders) out the door. We are now working toward the goal of increased sales. Then we spend the first part of the next month trying to recover from the inefficiency mess created near the end of the previous month. Obviously, from this example, we see that these goals are in conflict. At one time of the month we are working toward one goal, while at another time of the month we are working toward another goal. We can't achieve both goals simultaneously. As an additional explanation of this conflict, refer to your elementary economics class where you learned about the production function. This function taught us that the volume at which we produce to achieve maximum sales is not the same volume at which we produce to achieve maximum profits. So which is your goal: sales, profits, cost reductions, market share, or return on investment? Several are in conflict with each other. You can't have them all as your goal (unless you're happy with not really achieving any of them).

Able to allow for and encourage change. A well-developed world class goals system realizes that employees need to be able to interact with and initiate change (empowerment). They can't wait for change decisions to come from the top. They need to participate in the change process (participative management). Employees need to be prepared for change (training and education) and motivated toward change (measurement systems).

Simple but not simplistic. Goals should be simple; the shorter the better. Complex goals are harder to understand and are therefore ignored. Ideally, the vision portion of the goal should be short enough to be wall plaque material and easily remembered and stated by the employees. The vision should stress the core competency of the organization. The mission statement should also be simple, a collection of 10 or so sentences, stating how the vision can be operationalized. Similar rules apply to the strategies of the organization.

The vision, mission, and strategy should not be simplistic, like, "We want to get better" or "We want to get richer." These are too vague and employees have difficulty hanging their hat on them.

Precise. Goals need to be precise, especially as you get down into the strategies. Goal achievement needs to be measurable. An imprecise goal leads to confusion. The goal needs to be quantifiable and precisely related to each employee telling them what is expected of them.

Measurable. The enterprise needs competitive performance measures to make sure they are staying on top of the competition. Measures such as productivity, quality, time to market, and efficiency are excellent internal operational measures that demonstrate performance on a team basis. Measures on employee satisfaction and customer satisfaction are excellent departmental measures of performance. One important lesson about measurement systems that needs to be learned if we are to achieve world class status is that a measurement system does not exist for management information or for costing; it exists for motivation.

What you measure is what you motivate!

Don't measure or motivate labor efficiency if what you really want is materials efficiency. And don't measure or motivate labor efficiency if what you really want is quality. You'll receive results in what you measure, not in what you vocalize. And don't try to tell yourself that you can measure labor efficiency, materials efficiency, and quality all at the same time unless you want to

- confuse employees as to what you're really after, and
- receive average performance in each area as opposed to achieving excellent performance in the area that you really need performance in, which should be your critical resource.

A goal needs to be measured to ensure performance and goal achievement, and it needs to measure the right things to generate the proper motivation.

Uncompromised. A goal needs to be uncompromised. Once established, it needs to be committed to. This is one reason why goal ownership by the employees is so important. Wishy-washy management commitment to goal achievement results in non-achievement. This also refers to goal downsizing.

If the employees were involved in goal development, then if they don't achieve the goal we shouldn't go back and say, "Well, you did OK and we'll give you your bonus anyway." That will whitewash the goals and will result in poor goal setting in the future. Goals need to taken seriously and they need to be committed to!

Focused. Far too many companies operate similar to the one in Figure 10.2 and show a lack of focus. It is basically running the plant two different ways. Since the goals are in conflict, which measurement system is appropriate? The one used during the first 90 percent of the month would be efficiency, productivity, and cost of production; the measurement system used during the last 10 percent of the month would be a sales growth measure. Stressing both will result in the type of chaos shown in Figure 10.2. We need to have focus in our goals, which means we need a target that is well defined and challenging. Set your goal, build a measurement system around it, and stick to it.

Achievable yet challenging. The last characteristic of goal setting is that the goal should make us stretch ourselves but not kill ourselves. We don't want last year's performance to be next year's goal. We want the new goal to be significantly but realistically better than last year's accomplishments, thereby making us better.

Now that we have discussed the characteristics of good goals, let's discuss the role of secondary goals and then take a look at the implementation of a good set of goals. Earlier in this chapter we discussed multiple conflicting goals. We also mentioned that we need a single, focused target to shoot at. Does this mean that secondary goals are bad? Definitely not! Not as long as they don't conflict with or interfere with the primary goal. We can hit multiple targets if they are nicely laid on top of each other, but not if they are off in different directions. There is nothing wrong with having secondary goals as long as they strengthen, rather than conflict with, the primary goal. Let me give you an example. If your primary goal is employee permanence and stability, then it would be appropriate to ask what secondary goal would support this primary goal. If we want the employees to have jobs, then we want the plant to be around as long as possible. To do this we need to make sure we manufacture the product as long as possible. We need to control the market and the production of the product. An appropriate secondary goal would be to control market share. Then the next question is, how do we control market share? This may take a little price-cutting or gouging until you control the market. Then you can make the price whatever you want. But a more important way to control market share is by using the definition of quality discussed earlier, which is "to make a product the customer enjoys, likes, and appreciates so much that they wouldn't think of buying from anyone else." A recap of this chain of goals would be as follows:

- Primary goal: employee permanence and stability
- Secondary goal: control market share
- Tertiary goal: quality product

Another type of secondary goal is to break a goal down by departments or management levels. It would be helpful if each department was able to define a subgoal that would demonstrate its efforts toward the primary goal. This subgoal would be measurable within the organization and would be more useful to the specific organization than the primary goal.

Target Implementation

Figure 10.3 briefly outlines what the goal statements of an organization may look like. Note the focus on the core competencies and the strengthening of these core competencies by the development of goals around these. Also note the focus on goals and the development of supportive subgoals that will assist in the achievement of the primary goal.

As we implement the goals, we need to remember

- goal participation and ownership,
- employee preparation and training, and
- the corporate value system.

Goal participation and ownership. Again I need to stress that the most effective goal structure is a participative one,

VISION STATEMENT

- The vision statement is one or two sentences stating the long-term vision of the enterprise, focusing on the core competencies of the organization.

MISSION STATEMENT

- The mission statement is a series of goal statements indicating how the organization plans to achieve the vision.
- This statement specifies what areas the organization plans to change (become better), where it sees its strengths, and how it plans to develop these strengths.
- The mission should be measurable with a target completion date.
- The mission statement, like the vision, should focus on the core competencies of the enterprise.

STRATEGY

- The strategy is a focus on the various strategic areas and priorities of the organization.
- A strategy includes a quantifiable set of goals stating how each area plans to support and achieve the mission statement.

Figure 10.3 Goal development.

where the employees are involved in the setting of the goals and in the implementation of the goals. Only with employee participation do you achieve employee ownership. And only with employee ownership do we achieve a corporate-wide success commitment.

Employee preparation and training. It's one thing to set goals; it is entirely another thing to make sure that the employees have the tools necessary to achieve the goals. Sometimes this means technology, but often this means training. For example, if quality improvement is a goal, then the employees need to be trained in quality improvement tools: what they are, how to use them, and how they can make a difference. I know a company (name withheld to protect the innocent) that has been using statistical process tracking tools for many years to monitor quality. Recently, I was brought in and asked, "Why are we developing these control charts? What are we supposed to do with them?" Previous management had gotten on a quality control kick and had made employees fill out control charts. Most employees didn't know how to or why. They just did it because they were told to. Is it any surprise that quality didn't improve in spite of the quality control system?

The corporate value system. The corporate value system needs to be at the heart of all goals and their implementation. Goal achievement should incorporate values, not take a backseat to them. For example, honesty and integrity are often thrown to the wind to make the numbers look good. A company that loses its values to numbers will have a long road trying to get its lost integrity back. And, since the numbers weren't realistic anyway, it will also have trouble achieving its realistic goals.

With the necessary commitment and tools, employees will be eager and interested in driving the enterprise toward world class status.

When Goals Don't Work

If you don't follow the basics of goal development, goals are nothing more than plaques on the wall. For example, a recent survey of more than 300 electronics companies found that 63 percent had failed to improve quality defects by as much as 10 percent. The reason stated was that the programs were not "results driven"; they did not have goals that were measured and motivated within a specific time frame. Another example of failure are the many companies who have identified so many activities in so many places in the change process that it required a complex chart just to describe them all (we leave the name of the company out when the news is bad). In another case, successful change was measured by having 100 percent of the employees attending a quality-training program. I wonder if anyone cares if they learned anything.

In other cases failure occurred because credit wasn't given where credit was due; management sucked up all the credit for what the employees accomplished.

I was asked to visit the plant of a company that had been officially notified of closure. Since the plant was going to close anyway, the management wanted to know what went wrong. It didn't take long to discover a quality improvement system that had all the appropriate control charts and process control tools. The employee training was in place. The plaques about quality were on the wall. So what went wrong? What we quickly learned was that employee performance was measured based on units of output. No one was measured on quality improvements. And so no quality improvements occurred, primarily because quality changes would interfere with productive units produced, which meant that quality improvements would actually reduce, rather than increase, the bonus. The employees weren't dumb; they knew how to kiss up to the management fad of implementing quality control systems, while at the same time maintaining the quality of their paychecks. Another instance where goal achievement fails is when the principles and values of the enterprise and its employees are compromised to achieve the goals. This makes goal achievement a negative event, rather than an exciting and celebrated event.

Goal achievement can only occur based on the principles and characteristics outlined in this chapter. Otherwise, don't expect world class results!

The End State Statement

The end state is a reflection back on the visioning exercise of Chapter 9. Here the team is asked to look at the priority statement and discuss what the desired state would be for that priority. By visualizing the desired state of the priority, it then becomes easier to determine the gap that exists between the current state and this ideal future state. Understanding the future state as well as the gap makes it easier to identify goals for that priority.

Summarizing the Lessons Learned in This Chapter Using an Example

This chapter covered a large number of topics that define the development of the strategy map:

1. Core competencies
2. Vision
3. Mission
4. Defining the customer
5. Priorities and goals
   a. Priority statement
   b. End state statement
   c. Goals statement

It would now be useful to see a couple of examples of how this information should look as it gets generated.

Example 10.1

The first example will be for a high-tech organization like Dell, Cisco, Microsoft, Apple, Sony, or Motorola. These companies utilize contract manufacturers to build many of the products that they sell. They sell products through numerous channels including to customers directly, through resellers, through retail outlets, and others. They have internal processes that manage logistics, warehousing, planning, scheduling, inventory management, and so forth. For these extremely complex organizations, we could find a strategy map that contains something similar to the following:

1. Core competencies: Telecommunications
2. Vision: To provide the largest customer value-added content of any telecom organization in the world
3. Mission: To have the largest market share of any telecom company by 2020
4. Defining the customer: Retailers like Fry's and Best Buy, on-line direct-buy consumers, resellers like AT&T and Sprint
5. Priorities and goals
   a. Priority statement #1: An actively engaged and learning workforce
      i. End state statement: One improvement suggestion per employee per year and 70 percent

                of the workforce actively engaged in some type of training or education

    ii. Goals statement: By 2015, one improvement suggestion per employee every 2 years and 40 percent of the workforce actively engaged in some type of training or education; by 2020, one improvement suggestion per employee per year and 70 percent of the workforce actively engaged in some type of training or education

  b. Priority statement #2: Market dominance

    i. End state statement: Be a recognized market leader for 75 percent of our product lines

    ii. Goals statement: By 2015, become the most visible product at all retailers by having our product be the first product seen as customers enter the store; by 2020, be the dominant choice for all direct-buy customers—more hits on our direct-buy Web site than any of our competitors

  c. Priority statement #3: Product quality levels achieve 97 percent

    i. End state statement: Have our product name be synonymous with quality for all our products

    ii. Goals statement: By 2015, 90 percent defect-free and 95 percent on-time deliveries; by 2020, 97 percent defect-free and 99 percent on-time deliveries

Example 10.2

The second example will be for an oil and gas producer, like Shell, Mobil, or Exxon. These companies have several nearly independent elements to their business. For example, there is the exploration piece, the pumping of the oil, refining, distribution, and retail elements. They also sell products through numerous channels including to customers directly through their retail outlets like gas stations, through resellers, or to other manufacturers like plastics producers. Each of these branches of the business has internal processes that manage logistics, warehousing, planning, scheduling, inventory management, and so forth. For these extremely complex organizations, we could find a strategy map that contains something similar to the following:

1. Core competencies: Energy generation
2. Vision: To provide the most efficient and cost-effective sources of energy for all customers
3. Mission: To have the largest market share of any energy production company by 2020
4. Defining the customer: Retailer gas stations, plastics producers, reprocessors/remanufacturers who produce specialty fuel products
5. Priorities and goals
   a. Priority statement #1: Leading-edge innovator of new sources of cheaper energy
      i. End state statement: Diversified sources of energy available to all customers
      ii. Goals statement: By 2015, multiple (more than five) nonpolluting energy products that can be used as automotive fuel
   b. Priority statement #2: Market dominance
      i. End state statement: Be a recognized market leader for low-cost, quality energy resources
      ii. Goals statement: By 2015, identify cost reduction methodologies that will make energy generation cheaper for the consumer
   c. Priority statement #3: Improved customer responsiveness
      i. End state statement: Have our product name be synonymous with on-time delivery for all our products
      ii. Goals statement: By 2015, 95 percent on-time deliveries; by 2020, 99 percent on-time deliveries

These are quick and crude examples of how a strategy map should be populated. Most companies are more focused and have more specific and urgent priorities to deal with, but these examples will start the reader down the road toward identifying a realistic set of priorities for their particular organization.

Summary

This chapter has started the reader down the road of developing a strategy map (see Figure 10.1) for their organization. The following topics were covered, including examples, to define the development of the strategy map:

1. Core competencies
2. Vision
3. Mission
4. Defining the customer
5. Priorities and goals
    a. Priority statement
    b. End state statement
    c. Goals statement

The next chapters will build out even more of the strategy map that we saw in Figure 10.1, including

1. Objective/strategy statement
2. Metrics statements
3. Task/action item statements

After we have an understanding of these pieces of the strategy map, we will be ready to discuss the most important part of this book, the execution of the strategy.

11

Priority-Based Strategies/Metrics That Measure/Tasks

Driving Strategy to Execution

Organizational
Framework

1 –Trends
2 –Role
3 –Options
4 –Process

15 –Defining WC
16 –Conclusions

World Class
Status

5 –Culutre
6 –Alignment
7 –Metrics
8 –Integration

9 –Visioning
10 –Vision / Mission
11 –Priorities
12 –Governance
13 –Lean
14 –Repeat

Organizational
Performance

Strategy
Execution

Front-End Strategic Information			
Core Competencies:			
Vision:			
Mission:			
Defining the Customer:			
The Strategy Map			
Priorities and Goals:	Objectives / Strategies:	Metrics:	Tasks / Action Items:
Priority Statement: End State Statement:	Objective / Strategy Statement:	Metrics Statements:	Tasks / Action Item Statements:
Goal Statement:	Objective / Strategy Statement:	Metrics Statements:	Tasks / Action Item Statements:
	Objective / Strategy Statement:	Metrics Statements:	Tasks / Action Item Statements:

Figure 11.1 The strategy map.

> We must become the change we want to see.
>
> **—Mahatma Gandhi**

This chapter continues where the last chapter stopped in building a strategy map. Figure 11.1 is the same strategy format that we have seen in the previous chapters, but in this chapter we will focus on the last three columns of the lower half of the map. This is where we take our vision and mission statements and our priorities and goals and drill down on them, looking for a meaningful execution plan. We will go through this exercise by taking one priority at a time and developing it through the remaining three columns.

Objectives/Strategies

The second column of the map is often referred to by either of two names, Objectives or Strategies. Either name is appropriate. In this book, rather than using both names, we will refer to this column as the objectives.

The exercise of developing objectives starts with a close look at the Priorities column. We take the first priority and look at the corresponding End State and Goals, and ask questions like, What objectives need be executed to make an improvement on this priority? Often we have a tendency to start creating a long list of objectives. But we need to keep it down to five or fewer objectives per priority. We need to ask, What are the most dominant, key, highest value objectives that would drive us toward successfully achieving the goals defined with this priority?

We have a tendency to think that it should be easy to come up with a list of objectives. Nothing could be further from the truth. This task is not easy. Coming up with four or five focused objectives can be time consuming, especially if you are using a team effort, which is the correct way to identify these objectives.

This list of objectives is fluid. After the goals that have been tied to a particular priority have been met and new goals are developed, a new set of objectives is often also needed.

Objectives statements are brief action statements that describe what must be accomplished or changed so as to successfully achieve the intended results of the priority statement. Some basic rules for the development of objectives are as follows:

- A good objective communicates what strategic action must be accomplished to realize the intent of the priority.
- A good objective gives strategic direction on how to execute tasks (last column of the strategy map), which are the process improvements. It has a cause-and-effect relationship or linkage to other strategic objectives and priority statements.
- A good objective is easily measured and motivated by appropriate metrics, inspires and motivates the workforce to a higher level of performance, and drives significant operational change.
- A good objective is focused, easy to understand, memorable, executable, relevant, and concise.
- A good objective statement is seven words or fewer and starts with an action verb followed by a descriptive adjective and noun. Try to limit the length of each objective statement to seven words.

To help clarify the use of objective statements, here are a few examples of both good and bad objective statements:

- *Improve access to target markets.* This is not a good objective statement because it is not clear what is meant by *access* and who the target markets are.
- *Exploit learning technologies across the organization.* This is a good objective statement; it clearly describes what needs to be accomplished.
- *Understand gaining management's needs.* This is not a good objective statement because it lacks specific clarity on what is to be accomplished.
- *Reduce processing time by 20 percent.* This is a metric statement and not an objective statement.
- *Implement the software module in every division.* This is a task or an initiative and not an objective statement.
- *Right person, right place, and right time.* This is not a good objective statement; it provides no strategic direction and leaves the definition open as to what the word *right* should mean.
- *Improve the training and education of employees.* This is a good objective statement because it is understandable, executable, concise, and measurable.

Objective statements are often supported by definition statements, which add clarity to the objective. These objective definition statements capture the intent and purpose of each strategic objective statement. The objective definition statements make sure that the strategy map's strategic objective statements are understandable, executable, and enduring so they can be consistently communicated throughout the command. This ensures that the objective is communicated consistently and precisely. Objective definition statements would include the following elements:

- Three or four sentences that expand the meaning of the objective statement by defining the problem to be solved or the change to be implemented

- Sentences that highlight the root cause or reason behind the need for change
- Sentences that explain how the objective integrates and impacts the priority and the overall strategy map
- Precise clarification of why this objective is important for the target customers/stockholders and workforce

One final example of an objective statement and an objective definition statement follows:

> *Objective statement:* Attract, develop, and retain leading-edge talent
>
> *Objective definition statement:* Knowledgeable, experienced, and high-quality employees are the key to our organization's success. The objective is to reduce turnover and improve recruitment by creating a world class work environment built upon responsibility, clarity, personal motivation, satisfaction, and accountability. The objective is to provide all employees with the opportunity to directly impact the organization's performance and help it achieve its goals.

Metrics Statements

People respond to what is *inspected*, not what is *expected*.

Metrics are so important that we dedicated an earlier chapter to the topic (Chapter 7). As we learned, inaccurate metrics will influence and lead to inappropriate results. Metrics should not be chosen because they demonstrate visibility but rather so as to motivate a desired response.

Another metric tendency that must be avoided is the trend to identify large quantities of metrics in the hope that somewhere in the menagerie of metrics we will hit something meaningful. However, the lesson we have already learned is that having too many metrics is as ineffective as not having any metrics. Having too many metrics tends to be confusing, leaving the user frustrated rather than guided. Any more than three metrics per objective is too many, and the preferred number of metrics is one.

We need to find the metric that directly influences the behavior that we desire. Sometimes we know how reliable a metric is only after we have tested it over time.

Another important characteristic of a useful metric is to identify one that can be benchmarked and monitored. We need to have a starting value to know if we are getting any better. This starting value is the benchmark that we are working to improve. Then we need to be able to collect data on and monitor any changes to this metric.

Be careful not to stray too far from the goal statement that is listed with the priority statement. What this means is that the metrics in this column should focus on improvements that we are trying to achieve in the priority statement. For example, the goal statement in the first column probably has a metric associated with it. We need to make sure that the goal metric is aligned with the metrics statements listed in the third column. If these are not in sync, for example, if they are conflicting metrics, we may end up making the goal worse rather than moving closer toward achieving it.

Some basic rules for metrics are as follows:

- A metric must be the means to evaluate and communicate performance so the organization can see if the objective is being successfully implemented.
- A valid metric requires a current state benchmark for comparison and to demonstrate improvement.
- A metric focuses on how current performance needs to change or be improved (close performance gaps).
- A valid metric motivates the right behavior and action, which ultimately defines success.
- A valid metric includes a quantitative numeric unit of measure (number, percent, dollar amount, time, degrees, rankings, etc.).
- An effective metric is understandable, repeatable (eight words or fewer), and easy to calculate.

A first step in selecting metrics is to identify the critical success factors associated with each strategic objective. When selecting a metric we need to know what needs to change, be improved, or accomplished. Strategic metrics are the key to taking the entire strategy map away from the theoretical and turning it in to the practical, executable strategy. When metrics are correctly selected and used, the metric provides operational direction, aligns the workforce, improves decision making, serves as a basis for resource allocations, and verifies the validity and assumptions of the overall strategic plan.

Strategically focused metrics shift the analysis focus away from activities and toward outcomes. A strategic metric focuses on the process *value* created rather than on the process itself. Correctly selected strategic metrics communicate what needs to be accomplished to the workforce, thereby dramatically increasing performance and reducing costs.

The measure is an assessment of how well the organization accomplishes its critical success factors. For example, if the strategic objective is *better customer service* and the critical success factor is *prompt delivery*, the measure might be *cycle time from order placement to delivery*.

The goal isn't set up to monitor every action that could affect the desired outcome of an objective statement. It is used to identify those actions and support metrics that have a major influence on how well the objective is implemented.

An effective metric should satisfy the following criteria:

- *Focus on strategic communication.* The selected metric must adequately focus on the critical strategic issue. There must be a cause-and-effect impact on multiple strategic objectives and metrics throughout the strategy map.
- *Repeatable and reliable.* The metric must be quantifiable and meaningful for the employees who are responsible for achieving them.
- *Frequency of reporting.* The frequency of performance must be often enough to be able to change behavior. In some cases this means minute-by-minute updates.
- *Adequate target setting.* Meaningful targets for improvement should be established in the goal statements of the priority.
- *Assign accountability.* Accountability should be team based and not the responsibility of one individual.

Some examples of both good and bad metrics are as follows:

- *Number of hours of overtime.* This is a good metric because it is easy to understand, focuses on how current performance needs to change, and includes a quantitative numeric unit of measure.
- *Employee time spent on ancillary training.* This is a weak metric because it lacks focus on what specifically is being measured. For example, what defines *ancillary training*?
- *Performance effectiveness.* This is a bad metric because it is not understandable. What defines *performance*? How is it measured?
- *Reduce processing time by 20 percent.* This is a goal or an objective statement with a target, not a metric.
- *Number of safety incidents.* This would be a good metric as long as how to count *safety incidents* is understood.
- *Average time to fill an open position.* This is a bad metric because averages will always result in poor performance being offset with good performance. Averages do not provide specific information to know whether performance is good or bad. Averages don't highlight outliers.
- *Percent of employee hires taking more than 30 days.* This measure meets all criteria for a good metric.

Metrics can also confuse behavior. For example, a metric that on the surface appears to be a good metric can actually provide poor results. A couple of examples from the author's experience will demonstrate this.

- Aircraft departures are measured as departing on time as long as they leave the gate on schedule, regardless of how long it takes them before they actually take off. This metric results in aircraft being rushed out of the gate and being delayed on the tarmac, which is not what was intended by *departing on time*. The risk is that planes may not be fully serviced when they leave the gate, and customers may not enjoy sitting on the tarmac for long periods of time.

- Aircraft repair performance is measured by the number of repairs completed on time in a week. *On time* is defined as the standard amount of time it takes to do this repair. This metric causes employees to "cherry pick" the assignments, leaving the longer, riskier project for later. The risk is that critical or important repairs may be delayed for long periods of time.

It is necessary to carefully select metrics and consider all the positive and negative impacts that a metric may generate. A metric that seems effective in motivating one response may have a very negative effect and therefore be a poor metric for a different objective. Some guidelines in metric selection include the following:

- *Focus.* What should be accomplished to achieve a part of the objective's desired results or outcome?
- *Behavior or action.* What is the behavior or action change the workforce should achieve through the use of this metric? What other undesirable ancillary behaviors may result from this metric?
- *Performance gap.* What is the current performance gap that we are trying to correct? What is the goal of the priority?
- *Availability of data.* What data is available to be used in monitoring performance and where can the data be found? Do we have a starting benchmark that we can use to demonstrate improvement?
- *Metric selection.* What are the one or two metrics that we can use to create the correct strategic focus and motivate the appropriate and desirable actions?

The selection of appropriate metrics is more an art form than a science. Sometimes identifying the best metric becomes a trial-and-error effort. However, as we saw in Chapter 7, which discusses metrics, selecting the wrong metric can actually make the situation worse. Having no metric is better than having a wrong metric. But without the correct metric, your goal will never be achieved, nor will you ever be able to demonstrate success.

> If you are not keeping score, you are just practicing.

Tasks/Action Items

The last column also tends to have two names, Tasks or Action Items. For this book we will refer to them as tasks. The Task column is a list of executable steps that will be necessary if we are to accomplish the corresponding objective. This in turn is necessary if we are to improve our priority.

Tasks should—

- Provide the tactical direction and processes needed to achieve the objective's intended results.
- State the tactical actions or deliverables that will "move the needle" on the metric gauge.
- Be a list of specific identified actions or steps that need to be taken to accomplish the objective.
- Be concise, simple, and understandable action statements consisting of specific deliverables.

The task list may be quite long. If it stretches beyond four or five items, we will need to prioritize and sequence their execution. Some tasks may have a large influence in achieving the objective while others may have a much smaller role. An excellent tool for assessing and prioritizing the task list is the impact/effort matrix, which can be seen in Figure 11.2.

In Figure 11.2 we see *impact* plotted on the vertical axis and *effort* plotted on the horizontal axis. Task 1 is high in the level of impact and low in the level of effort. Task 8 is low in impact and high in effort. The tasks in the upper left quadrant (tasks 1, 6, and 2) would be executed first, followed by the tasks in the upper right quadrant (tasks 4, 5, and 7), followed by the

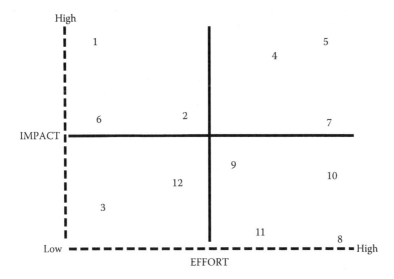

Figure 11.2 Impact/effort matrix.

tasks in the bottom left quadrant (tasks 3 and 12). The tasks in the bottom right quadrant may never be executed because the effort isn't worth the benefit (tasks 8, 9, 10, and 11).

Most organizations do not have unlimited resources and would have to prioritize which tasks they execute and in which order. With this prioritization technique we now have the necessary prioritized task list, and we would execute the tasks based on this prioritization.

An Example

Figure 11.3 offers a somewhat silly example of what a strategy map could look like. Your strategy map should include multiple priorities, each with their corresponding goals and end state statements, and each with a set of objectives, metrics, and corresponding tasks. Also, for space considerations, I have left out the objective definition statements. From this example you can see how easy it is to design a strategy map. As we've already discussed, the difficulty comes in making it executable.

Front-End Strategic Information			
Core Competencies: World Class Leading Edge Scientific Expertise			
Vision: The Advancement of Science in the United States			
Mission: Send a team to Mars and return them safely to Earth in the next decade			
Defining the Customer: The American People			
The Strategy Map			
Priorities and Goals:	Objectives / Strategies:	Metrics:	Tasks / Action Items:
Priority Statement: Build a rocket with the capability of Mars travel	**Objective Statement:** Engineer a ship with the capability of taking passengers to Mars	**Metrics:** Time required to design resources required	**Tasks:** Identify the engineering resources that will be needed to accomplish
End State Statement: A successfully designed and executed mission to Mars	**Objective Statement:** Train a team of astronauts for a Mars mission	**Metrics:** Time required to train Number of astronauts that will need training	**Tasks:** Define the critical mass of astronauts needed to end up with the crew
Goal Statement: By the year 2022 the first mission to Mars will be completed	**Objective Statement:** Identify the Manufacturing capability for constructing the Mars rocket	**Metrics:** Time required to prepare to manufacture Time required to manufacture	**Tasks:** Detailed survey of manufacturing capability Selection of the manufacturer

Figure 11.3 The strategy map example.

Summary

This chapter has continued the process of defining and developing the strategy map. It has continued where the last chapter left off by focusing on the last three columns of the lower half of the map. This is where we have taken our vision and mission statements and our priorities and goals and have drilled down on them looking for a meaningful execution plan. We go through this exercise by taking one priority at a time and developing it through the remaining three columns:

- Objective or Strategy Statement (including the Objective Definition Statement)
- Metrics
- Tasks or Action Item Statements

Next we will focus on structuring a governance methodology around each of these, which will allow for the successful execution of the organizational strategy.

12

Governance/ Performance Reviews/ Cascading/ Communication

Driving Strategy to Execution

Organizational Framework

1 –Trends
2 –Role
3 –Options
4 –Process

5 –Culture
6 –Alignment
7 –Metrics
8 –Integration

Organizational Performance

World Class Status

15 –Defining WC
16 –Conclusions

9 –Visioning
10 –Vision / Mission
11 –Priorities
12 –Governance
13 –Lean
14 –Repeat

Strategy Execution

In the previous chapters we constructed a strategy map. Preferably this would be done using a team of the organization's leadership. Next we address what needs to be accomplished to successfully support the execution of the strategy map and to ensure that it continues as a relevant strategic planning document. In this chapter we will discuss the steps necessary to execute this map:

- *Governance plan.* Governance focuses on accountability and on keeping the strategy map in the forefront of all management's efforts.
- *Performance reviews.* We will discuss strategic performance reviews and how they should be executed. These reviews allow management to monitor the results of their strategy plan and to make adjustments as needed.
- *Cascading the strategy map throughout the organization.* In this step of cascading, the high-level strategy map is dissected and brought down to the level of each division or department so that each can see the piece of the strategy pie that belongs to them. It gives the lower levels the accountability and ownership they need.
- *Communicating the information on the strategy map.* This requires enacting an aggressive organization-wide strategy communication plan that continuously provides updates on how the strategic plan is being implemented. It provides feedback from the individuals who are executing parts of the strategic plan in their areas of responsibility.

Governance Plan

Governance is a fancy term for accountability. With governance we are establishing a plan whereby management can check on the progress that is being made on the priorities. Metrics are checked and the execution of tasks is validated. By using governance reporting tools, management keeps the strategy map visible throughout the entire organization at the forefront of all management's efforts.

Gaining an understanding of governance facilitates achieving a quality strategy execution. Strategy governance is the management process for making decisions based on the actual results. These results become visible through the metrics. Metrics are impacted by the internal and external influences (threats and opportunities) that affect strategic performance, which in turn are affected by implementing specific operational tasks.

The primary purpose of a governance plan can be listed with the following key points:

- Strategic governance controls and monitors the execution of strategic plans.
- Strategic governance monitors, adjusts, and aligns the strategy map as needed to keep it relevant.
- Strategic governance prioritizes and optimizes an organization's critical resources (doing the right things at the right time).
- Strategic governance keeps the strategy map as the centerpiece of strategic decision making.
- Strategic governance builds accountability throughout the organization.
- Strategic governance ensures leadership accountability and workforce involvement.

The strategy performance reviews (SPRs, also discussed below in the "Performance Reviews" section) become the centerpiece for reporting the results of strategic decision making and strategy execution. Strategic decision making is never static. It will always be impacted by the constant flow of new internal and external information. Effective strategy governance facilitates flexible and fast response to change.

The critical success indicators of strategy governance are

- *Accountability.* Who is responsible for what task? Is it on track, on schedule, achieving the desired results? Leadership validates that their plans have not been sidetracked by extraneous issues.
- *Focus.* Are we staying focused on the priorities that we identified as the most critical for our success? Strategy

map analysis has changed how operational decisions are made.

- *Teamwork.* Are the various elements of the organization working together toward achieving the identified goals? The work culture of the organization has changed. It should be easier to learn, share, and grow in strategic and operational knowledge.
- *Results.* Are we moving the needle on the metrics appropriately? There should be an increase in team-based innovative and "outside of the box" creative thinking.

Governance also includes an overview of how the strategy map will be deployed and cascaded through the organization. When a strategy governance process is put into practice, the focus of the organization changes. There will now be a concerted effort within the organization to focus on executing high-impact strategic priorities and their corresponding goals. Strategic execution feedback (or information roll-up) will consistently be coming from the employees as they implement strategy.

Performance Reviews

In this section we will discuss the criteria for a successful performance review, often referred to as the strategy performance review or SPR briefing. We will also see how strategic objective performance needs to be managed and evaluated by *objective champions.*

Successfully facilitated SPRs will collaboratively achieve the following outcomes:

- Create an opportunity for dialogue between the various parts of the organization that are affected by a particular objective or priority
- Open the door to find new insights in achieving the stated goals
- Create an opportunity for analyzing performance results
- Engage in integrated-team problem solving

- Create opportunities to devise and evaluate strategic initiatives and tasks
- Improve performance management
- Create the opportunity to continually assess external and internal environments and events that impact execution of strategic priorities

To achieve these desired SPR meeting results, senior leadership will need to keep the attendees focused on the strategic objectives and not on day-to-day operations. Management needs to create an environment that promotes candor in sharing ideas to foster a sense of common purpose. Attendees need to be encouraged to think beyond their own job responsibilities.

Since ownership and accountability are critical to the successful deployment of a strategy map, often objective champions are assigned to each of the objectives on the map. The objective champion becomes responsible for the execution of that particular objective and reports on the performance of their objective during the SPR meetings. Objective champions are assigned by management and need to have the authority (and budget) to successfully drive the objective to completion.

Objective champions are not necessarily individuals that are directly involved in the focus area of the objective, but they normally are. However, some organizations specifically identify objective champions that are outside of the focus area of the objective, thereby hoping to bring in an outsider's perspective and a new set of ideas. Objective champions become a vital part of the execution of the strategy map. Objective champions need to understand their key roles and responsibilities.

Effective SPR meetings are dependent on the objective champion's clearly understanding and accepting their responsibilities associated with the objective. They need to understand the desired outcomes of the strategic objectives. The responsibilities of an objective champion include the following:

- Developing and coordinating action plans and tasks (the same tasks that are in the fourth column of the strategy map) that lead the organization's workforce to deliver the strategic objective's targeted results

- Prioritizing the tasks and identifying resources to achieve the tasks
- Establishing a team to promote cross-function integration of activities that support the objective's planning, execution, and performance
- Reviewing how other strategic objectives are impacting the performance of the strategic objective being assessed
- Identifying performance measures (the third column of the strategy map) and creating short- and long-term stretch targets
- Analyzing the metrics for trends, barriers, effectiveness, and efficiency improvements that lead to removing the obstacles that inhibit progress
- Delivering a performance assessment of your objective at SPR strategy review briefings

The following are some guidelines that can be used when assessing and reporting on a strategic objective's purpose, obstacles, action plans, and milestones. The reporting needs to stay focused on the most critical issues that address the areas of most interest for the briefing attendees. The following four points should be addressed during the objective champion's strategic objective assessment report:

- *Problems or issues.* What are the fundamental problems or opportunities for improvement that need to be addressed to advance the intended results of the strategic objective? Is the strategic objective still relevant to the priority, and will its implementation have strategic value? Or have new, higher priority objectives taken its place with respect to the priority? The objective champion needs to be able to define what success will look like after the intended results of the strategic objective are achieved.
- *Analysis.* What are the root causes, both internal and external, of the problems or opportunities that are impacting the implementation of the objective? What can be done to improve performance and eliminate barriers? The objective champion and his team identify the

obstacles and risks that need to be overcome for successful execution of the strategic objective.

- *Action Plan*. What specific tasks have been identified as necessary for the execution of this objective? What action plans and initiatives have been established to execute those tasks? What Lean or Six Sigma (see Chapter 13) events are being executed to achieve the intended results? Are the right activities being selected, funded, and staffed? The objective champion should focus on defining how the intended results of the strategic objective are achieved.
- *Milestones*. What specific time-stamped milestones have been established? The objective champion defines how the action plans will be monitored. This determines if they are effectively and efficiently achieving the intended results of the strategic objective.

The SPR meeting can occur weekly, monthly, or quarterly depending on the required level of management control. The SPR uses the strategy map as the foundational tool to communicate strategic plans and offer strategic direction during the meetings. Strategy performance should be reviewed using three primary reporting documents during SPR: the Scorecard Report, the Dashboard Report, and the Problem-Solving Status Report.

Scorecard Report

A Scorecard Report is a summary of the strategy map's objective statements, some key metrics, actual results, forecasted results, and corresponding stretch targets.

During the SPR, the first part of the objective champion's briefing should address her section of the results of the Scorecard Report. For example, the objective champion of Objective 1.1 (Table 12.1) should review the line associated with her objective. Reviewing the Scorecard Report will allow the objective champion to remind the strategy review briefing attendees of the purpose and critical success factors in implementing that strategic objective. The champion's review should answer the following questions:

TABLE 12.1
Sample Scorecard Report

Priorities and Their Objectives	Metrics	Previous Results	Current Results	Current Forecast	6-Mo. Forecast	12-Mo. Forecast	3-Year Target
			1.0 Priority #1				
1.1 First Objective under Priority #1	Critical metric under Objective 1.1	#s from the last reporting cycle	#s from the current cycle	What we predicted for the current cycle	Our prediction for 6 months out	Our prediction for 1 year out	Our prediction for 3 years out
1.2 Second Objective under Priority #1	Critical metric under Objective 1.2		Color code this box: Green = on or above target Yellow = below target but getting better Red = below target				
1.3 Third Objective under Priority #1	Critical metric under Objective 1.3						

2.0 Priority #2

2.1 First Objective under Priority # 2

First critical metric under Objective 2.1

Second critical metric under Objective 2.1

Third critical metric under Objective 2.1

Etc.

Etc.

- What describes the purpose and intent of the strategic objective?
- What has changed since the last report? What have we learned? How will this new information impact future progress?
- Did we achieve our commitments?
- Are we getting the results we wanted?
- Are operational adjustments being made?

The Scorecard Report will be populated by the objective champions. The data needs to be collected by their teams and listed on the Scorecard Report. The Scorecard Report needs to be updated at least one week prior to each SPR briefing. Some organizations prefer to have their Scorecard Reports updated regularly, often on a weekly basis.

Everyone should have access to the Scorecard Report. Some organizations even display it in a public and open location. It is recommended that everyone have at least limited access to the Scorecard Report.

During the SPR, when the Scorecard Report is presented, the use of drill-down slides will help to facilitate the understanding of a specific point or problem. The Dashboard Report or the Problem Solving Status Report will help to add clarification to any specific problems or issues.

Dashboard Report

The Dashboard Report (Table 12.2) is a summary of all the operational metrics listed in the strategy map and is used to monitor critical core processes.

The Dashboard Report has several purposes:

- Facilitates a deep dive into all the metrics related to a specific objective
- Allows the objective champion to monitor the progress and performance of his specific objective
- Serves as the ongoing tracking document for the metrics related to a specific objective
- Provides the scorecard metrics to be populated from the data on this report

TABLE 12.2
Sample Operational Dashboard Report

Priorities and Their Objectives	Status	Metrics	Baseline Start Date	Actual Target	Current Forecast	Forecast	Forecast	End Date Forecast
				1.0 Priority #1				
1.1 First Objective under Priority #1	Color code this box: Green = on or above target Yellow = below target but getting better Red = below target	First metric under Objective 1.1 (all metrics need to be included)	Value of this metric from the start of the project	Show the actual values for each month since the start of the project (multiple columns)	What the current value of this metric is	Blank	Blank	Estimated end date of the project
			Start date of the project	Show the target value	What we predicted for the current cycle	Our prediction for 6 months out (multiple columns)	Predictions (cont.)	Estimated forecast for the completion of the objective
		Second metric under Objective 1.1						
		Third metric under Objective 1.1						

Continued

TABLE 12.2
Sample Operational Dashboard Report

Priorities and Their Objectives	Status	Metrics	Baseline Start Date	Actual Target	Current Forecast	Forecast	Forecast	End Date Forecast
1.2 Second Objective under Priority #1		All metrics under Objective 1.2						
1.3 Third Objective under Priority #1		All metrics under Objective 1.3						
				2.0 Priority #2				
2.1 First Objective under Priority #2		First metric under Objective 2.1						
		Second metric under Objective 2.1						
		Third metric under Objective 2.1						
Etc.		Etc.						

Each objective champion may have their own dashboard, or it may be an automated tool that is kept in a central location. The Dashboard Report should not be reviewed in detail during the SPR briefings unless there is a question about a specific objective or metric.

Problem-Solving Status Report

The main purpose of the Problem-Solving Status Report is to provide a detailed review of the steps being implemented to ensure the strategic objective is executed correctly, but it is also used to highlight results and to indicate where there are execution problems.

Numerous documents can be used for problem-solving analysis and reporting. The author recommends the use of the A3 document, which is a tool developed by Toyota for the analysis and reporting of all projects. An example of an A3 can be seen in Figure 12.1. From this we see nine specific steps:

1. Clarify and validate the problem
2. Perform a purpose expansion on the problem
3. Break down the problem/identify performance gaps
4. Set improvement targets
5. Determine the root cause
6. Develop an improvement task list
7. Execute improvement tasks
8. Confirm results
9. Standardize successful process

From this you can see that Steps 1 through 3 are about clearly defining the problem or opportunity being worked on. Step 4 is about setting improvement targets for the problem area. Steps 5 and 6 are about making sure you're working on the right root cause and identifying the tasks that will be needed to solve the problem. Steps 7 and 8 track the improvement process and report the results. And Step 9 is about sharing the knowledge gained from this improvement process with other relevant areas of the business.

Every objective on the strategy map should have a corresponding 9-Step A3 prepared for it. Then, the information in

Team Members: **Who are the individuals who worked on this 9-step report?**	9-Step Opportunity (Problem) Analysis Tool	Approval Information/Signatures **Who are the champions for (signers of) this project?**
1. Clarify & Validate the Problem State the basic overall fundamental problem that needs to be solved and validate that it is strategically aligned with the enterprise objectives. **2. Perform a Purpose Expansion** on the Problem Confirm that we are doing the right things.	**5. Determine Root Cause** Define the root-causes of the current problem and the reason for current performance gaps. What caused the need for this change?	**7. Execute Improvement Tasks** Prioritize the actions listed in step 6, time sequence them, identify specific completion dates, assign responsibility for the completion, and state where help is needed in order to complete the action. What are the deliverables and their due dates?
3. Break Down the Problem/Identify Performance Gaps What are the facts? List what specifically needs to change to solve the problem and what are the performance gaps to be closed to realize required performance. Prove it!	**6. Develop Improvement Task List** List the specific actions that need to be implemented to create change and close performance gaps. Validate that all the root causes listed in step 5 have been accounted for and resolved. What needs to change in order to eliminate the root cause?	**8. Confirm Results** Report progress made on the improvement targets listed in step 4. Confirm that we are doing the right things in the right way by improving the desired performance areas. Did you achieve your desired results? (At-a-glance status)
4. Set Improvement Targets Set improvement targets. Identify annual and long term stretch targets as appropriate.		**9. Standardize Successful Processes** List ways to institutionalize best practices and processes learned from implementing this change. How can we institutionalize this "best practice?"

Figure 12.1 Nine-Step A3 with definitions.

Step 6 becomes the task list of the strategy map. The information in Step 4 ties to the metrics of the strategy map. Step 8 ties to the Dashboard and the Scorecard.

The A3 report is used to

- Provide detailed documentation about the project and its current state of performance
- Provide documentation support of the Dashboard and the Scorecard
- Provide drill-down information (if required) during the SPR review meeting

A detailed explanation of how to use the A3 report can be found in another book by the author, *Lean Management Principles for Information Technology* (CRC Press, 2011).

Wrap-Up Discussion on the SPR

A successful SPR will have the following characteristics:

- It will encourage continual feedback.
- It will review and monitor progress of the execution of strategic plans.
- It will analyze internal and external obstacles and risks to be overcome in achieving strategic outcomes.
- It will focus on the reasons for performance gaps and search for ways to eliminate the gaps.
- It will unify leadership to drive strategic change in achieving operational excellence and mission priorities.

Some of the logistics that surround an SPR include the following:

- *Frequency.* All of the strategy objectives on the strategy map need to be reviewed regularly. Some organizations have chosen to review all the objectives associated with a priority on a weekly basis. Since they have four priorities, each objective gets reviewed one a month, in rotation. Other organizations choose to do all the objectives once a month in one big meeting (usually about 4 hours). After the process becomes engrained into the organization, some organizations choose to meet only quarterly for an SPR.
- *Duration.* The monthly or quarterly SPR briefing should not last more than 4 hours. The weekly approach would split the 4 hours into a 1 hour meeting each week.
- *Integration into existing meetings.* Due to the holistic approach used in analyzing the strategic plans during the SPR briefing, most organizations find it redundant to hold other similar operational briefings and choose to eliminate them.

Cascading the Strategy Map

Cascading refers to sharing the information down the organizational food chain and making it relevant to the suborganizations. For example, the corporate strategy map will have several priorities and objectives. All those priorities and objectives may not be relevant to every department. Cascading, at the department level, refers to taking those objectives that are relevant and defining how the department will facilitate and execute toward that objective.

Cascading focuses on executing the strategy at the front lines of the organization. The goals of cascading are to

- Align and validate the strategy map at all organizational levels
- Develop a strategic "line of sight" between the organization's strategic objectives and tasks and employee responsibilities
- Promote workforce feedback on how to improve strategy execution
- Focus constrained resources on the prioritized strategic tasks and initiatives at the right time and in the right place

Effective strategy execution requires the cascading of corporate strategy to the lower levels of the organization. This ensures that the headquarters-level plans are translated into the plans of the various operating and support units. This is accomplished by executing lower level strategic initiatives and tasks that deliver on the corporate strategic plan. This will also align employees' competency development plans and their personal goals with the high-level strategic plans. When cascading is implemented, bridges will be created between an organization's strategy and its processes, systems, and people, which will ignite breakthrough results and generate effective and efficient strategy execution. Cascading creates focus and coordination across even the most complex organizations, thereby making it easier to identify and realize synergies.

Strategy cascading is accomplished by communicating strategy maps, Scorecards, Dashboards, and Problem-Solving Status Reports through the various levels of the organization. The cascaded information should be aligned with the higher level strategy maps. It should also reflect the unique operations of the lower level units and promote local ownership of the strategic plan.

An element of the cascading process is to hold cross-functional team meetings focused on the local relevant objectives. These meetings will serve the following purposes:

- Find new insights in the analysis of performance results
- Identify problem areas, performance gaps, and areas for improvement
- Generate opportunities for integrated team problem solving
- Create action plans and task lists
- Facilitate process improvements

With active operational cascading and integration, organizations will not establish local competing strategic priorities and be wasting limited resources on redundant or nonpriority tasks. When all elements of an organization are aligned around common critical strategic priorities, meeting customer needs will be greater than the sum of its individual separate units.

Communication Plan

Effective communication is 20 percent what you know and 80 percent how you feel about what you know.

—David Norton

The strategy map is a communication tool that depicts an organization's priorities, goals, and objectives. It allows leadership and the workforce to discuss strategic direction and to coordinate how best to realize deliverables. It instills accountability and reinforces the need to collaborate to achieve the highest possible performance success. When the strategy map is used as a communication tool, the workforce makes strategy execution part of their responsibility.

The goals of a communication plan are as follows:

- Communicate the organization's strategic plan and performance results
- Advance the organization's strategy by aligning the employees behind the plan
- Energize employees by aligning their work to applicable critical strategic objectives and tasks from the strategy map
- Empower employees to get the right things done correctly, thereby realizing major performance improvements
- Motivate employees to understand that they are the front line in successful strategy execution

A critical success factor in implementing strategy for any organization is that the right message is being understood and believed by the right people. Organizations that have a formal communication program dramatically outperform organizations that don't. If people do not understand the organization's strategic plan or do not see a way they can contribute to its success, it is the same as the organization having no strategic plan at all. Some additional goals of an effective strategy communication plan are as follows:

- To educate and motivate the entire staff about the strategy processes and to identify its operational value
- To develop a working understanding of the strategy map's components, allowing the workforce to know how it will impact their individual job responsibilities
- To create commitment and momentum among the workforce to support the execution of the strategic plan
- To promote workforce feedback on how to accomplish the goals of the selected strategic objectives and achieve breakthrough operational results

Effective communication to the workforce about strategy, targets, and initiatives is vital if the entire workforce is to contribute to the success of the strategy. This requires an understanding of the organization's strategy map, Scorecard, Dashboard, and Problem-Solving Status Report in all operating units and support functions. One of the most effective communication channels is having each employee hear about strategy directly from his or her management.

Components of an effective communication plan should include the following considerations:

- What is the key message that is being communicated?
- Who is the target audience?
- What are the media channels that will be used to share the message?
- How often is the message shared?
- Who has primary responsibility for making sure that the communication goes forward?

People who are knowledgeable and inspired by their organization's strategic plan will align their work responsibilities around strategic priorities. Then the workforce is in a better position to identify efficient ways to support the intended outcomes of the strategic plan.

Aligned and integrated strategy maps yield significant operational value when they are continuously communicated to the workforce and related to their job responsibilities. Successful communication initiatives use a variety of tools such as organizational briefings, newsletters, videos, Web sites, "Town Hall" meetings, new employee orientation programs, and one-on-one coaching. Communication plan outcomes include

- Unity and momentum among the entire workforce around a common strategic destination
- Senior leadership's continual commitment and passion to achieve the strategic plan
- Promoting work culture changes so it is easier to learn, share, and grow in knowledge
- Encourage innovative and "outside-of-the-box" creative thinking
- Build a foundation for strategic understanding, acceptance, execution, and ultimately breakthrough results

Successful communication is dependent on the right messages being understood and believed by the right people.

—Peter Drucker

Summary

In this chapter we addressed what needs to be accomplished to successfully support the execution of the strategy map that we built. The goal is to ensure that the map is sustainable and continues as a relevant strategic planning document. This chapter discussed the steps necessary to execute this map, which include

- A governance plan
- Performance reviews
- A plan for cascading the strategy map
- A plan for communicating the information on the strategy map

Now we are ready to execute the tasks that were identified in the last column of the strategy map. The execution requires a change mechanism, and the change mechanism that we recommend in this book will be Lean. So let's move forward and make the change.

13

"Moving the Needle" by Executing with Lean/Six Sigma

Driving Strategy to Execution

Organizational
Framework

World Class
Status

1 – Trends
2 – Role
3 – Options
4 – Process

15 – Defining WC
16 – Conclusions

5 – Culture
6 – Alignment
7 – Metrics
8 – Integration

9 – Visioning
10 – Vision / Mission
11 – Priorities
12 – Governance
13 – Lean
14 – Repeat

Organizational
Performance

Strategy
Execution

Front-End Strategic Information			
Core Competencies:			
Vision:			
Mission:			
Defining the Customer:			
The Strategy Map			
Priorities and Goals:	Objectives / Strategies:	Metrics:	Tasks / Action Items:
Priority Statement: End State Statement: Goal Statement:	Objective / Strategy Statement:	Metrics Statements:	Tasks / Action Item Statements:
	Objective / Strategy Statement:	Metrics Statements:	Tasks / Action Item Statements:
	Objective / Strategy Statement:	Metrics Statements:	Tasks / Action Item Statements:

Figure 13.1 The strategy map.

This chapter is both exciting and fun. In this chapter we make improvements. We get out of the business of making pretty charts and start implementing and executing the strategy that we've been discussing for the last 12 chapters. This is where we see a difference—where we see the metrics improve. We start with the task list that we developed in the fourth column of the strategy map (highlighted in Figure 13.1).

The tool that the authors recommend for this improvement process is Lean. However, it is impossible in one chapter to describe perfectly how Lean should work. Rather than trying to teach you how to do Lean, this chapter assumes that the reader has a basic understanding of Lean principles and how to apply them. This chapter will focus on linking the strategy map to the improvement principles provided by Lean.

If a more thorough understanding of Lean is required, there are a couple of books that the authors recommend. The first is *Reinventing Lean: Introducing Lean into the Supply Chain,* by Gerhard Plenert. This book goes through the fundamentals principles of Lean and how it is implemented. A second book, *Lean Management Principles for Information Technology,* also by Gerhard Plenert, provides the fundamentals of how a

Lean project should be managed using the A3 reporting tool, which was referred to in Chapter 12. With these two books, and with a little practice, the reader can become an expert Lean facilitator.

Lean Definition

There has always been a lot of interest in the Toyota Production System (TPS) tools, especially in Lean. It's hard to avoid hearing about all the successes that Lean has accomplished. From these discussions we learn that implementing Lean methodologies accomplishes the following and even more:

- Eliminates waste
- Reduces cycle and flow time
- Increases capacity
- Reduces inventories
- Increases customer satisfaction
- Eliminates bottlenecks
- Improves communication

So what is this mysterious tool referred to as *Lean*?

Lean is the Westernization of a Japanese concept known by several names. It's been known as the Toyota Production System (TPS), JIT (Just in Time), pull manufacturing, TQM (total quality management), and other names. Each of these methodologies incorporates some aspects of Lean. What we know as Lean today has grown to become more than any of these. One possible definition of Lean, taken from MainStream Management, a Lean consulting company, is as follows:

> Lean is a systematic approach that focuses the entire enterprise on continuously improving quality, cost, delivery, and safety by seeking to eliminate waste, create flow, and increase the velocity of the system's ability to meet customer demand. Lean today has become a collection of tools and methodologies, very few of which are actually "required" in any specific Lean process. When working on a specific Lean project, the role of a Lean facilitator is to design and assemble the correct mix of tools to optimally facilitate the desired

result. For example, if the goal is to improve cycle time, the facilitator would assemble one set of tools; an entirely different set of tools would be used if we were trying to improve quality.

Lean has developed into its own entity, and along with that, it has developed its own award process, the Shingo Prize for Excellence in Manufacturing. In fact, the Shingo award program has become the international standard for what Lean should look like.

Lean is also about team building, integration, and ownership. The Lean facilitator is tasked with organizing the appropriate teams and then giving them the guidance and training necessary in the selected tools so that the Lean effort can progress with the greatest efficiency. The team makes the decisions about any changes in process and has ownership of these changes. It is the role of the facilitator to keep the team on track so that they develop and implement these changes in the minimal amount of time.

Executing Using Lean

The strategy map contains the guiding principles that we follow as we migrate through the change process. The last column of the strategy map contains the list of tasks that we need to execute to accomplish the desired improvements. As mentioned previously, this list of tasks needs to be prioritized. The strategy report task list often results in a large number of tasks. Generally we do not have the resources to execute all of the tasks simultaneously. Therefore it becomes necessary to prioritize these tasks and determine which ones should be executed first. A tool that is commonly used for prioritization is the effort/impact matrix. Using this tool we look at each task and plot it on the chart based on the impact that the task has on the overall organization and the effort (level of resources and time) that will be required to implement the task. The tasks that appear the furthest toward the upper left corner should be the low-hanging fruit that is implemented first. The sequence should be to do the tasks in the upper left quadrant,

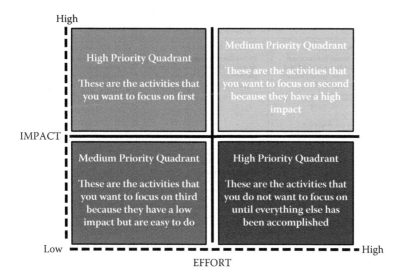

Figure 13.2 Impact/effort matrix.

then the upper right, then the lower left, and last of all the lower right, which will probably never get executed. The effort/impact matrix was previously referred to in Chapter 11 (see Figure 13.2).

After the activities have been prioritized into the four quadrants, we can now move forward in executing each of the tasks, starting first with the highest priority tasks. We take the selected task and start to analyze the task by filling in the first four steps of the A3 (see Figure 13.3).

1. *Clarify and validate the problem.* Do we understand the problem enough to define it?
2. *Perform a purpose expansion on the problem.* What is the purpose of solving this problem? Validate that there is a strategic linkage.
3. *Break down the problem/verify performance gaps.* Do we understand the problem well enough to break it down? What is the performance issue that we are trying to improve?
4. *Set improvement targets.* Where should our performance be after the improvements have been implemented?

Team Members: Who are the individuals who worked on this 9-step report?	9-Step Opportunity (Problem) Analysis Tool	Approval Information/Signatures Who are the champions for (signers of) this Project?
1. Clarify & Validate the Problem State the basic overall fundamental problem that needs to be solved and validate that it is strategically aligned with the enterprise objectives.	**5. Determine Root Cause** Define the root-causes of the current problem and the reason for current performance gaps. What caused the need for this change?	**7. Execute Improvement Tasks** Prioritize the actions listed in step 6, time sequence them, identify specific completion dates, assign responsibility for the completion, and state where help is needed in order to complete the action. What are the deliverables and their due dates?
2. Perform a Purpose Expansion on the Problem Confirm that we are doing the right things.		
3. Break Down the Problem/Identify Performance Gaps What are the facts? List what specifically needs to change to solve the problem and what are the performance gaps to be closed to realize required performance. Prove it!	**6. Develop Improvement Task List** List the specific actions that need to be implemented to create change and close performance gaps. Validate that all the root causes listed in step 5 have been accounted for and resolved. What needs to change in order to eliminate the root cause?	**8. Confirm Results** Report progress made on the improvement targets listed in step 4. Confirm that we are doing the right things in the right way by improving the desired performance areas. Did you achieve your desired results? (At-a-glance status)
4. Set Improvement Targets Set improvement targets. Identify annual and long term stretch targets as appropriate.		**9. Standardize Successful Processes** List ways to institutionalize best practices and processes learned from implementing this change. How can we institutionalize this "best practice?"

Figure 13.3 Nine-Step A3 with definitions.

The exercise of filling in the Steps 1–4 of the 9-Step Opportunity Analysis tool, or A3, will define the complexity and effort that will be required to resolve the task. Any of the following may result from this analysis:

1. The task may be too complex, and we may need to break the task down further into subtasks, each of which is executed separately.
2. The task may need to be executed through a RIE (rapid improvement event).
3. The task may be simplistic (referred to as a "just-do-it") and is executed immediately.
4. The task may require resources or involvement beyond the scope of this champion and may need to be escalated to a higher level of authority.

In the case of 1, 3, or 4, the process basically stops. In the case of option 1, we will repeat the A3 analysis process for each of the resulting subtasks, just as if it was a task of its own. In option 3 we simply do the task and move forward toward the next task. In option 4, the task is out of scope until a new, higher level champion has been identified with the authority to proceed.

Assuming we are dealing with option 2, we now execute a RIE on this task. The RIE is a Lean event where we get a team of subject matter experts together and discuss the problem in detail. The first objective of the RIE is to get a clear understanding of the root causes of the problem. This fills in Step 5 of the A3 document where we analyze the root cause of the problem using tools like the fishbone chart, the five whys, or affinity diagrams (again, the book *Lean Management Principles for Information Technology* does an excellent job of explaining each of these).

The second objective of the RIE is to get a clear understanding of the current state of the problem and then to design a desired future state. The tool used for the RIE is value stream mapping. Once we understand the current and desired future state, the gaps between the two help us design the tasks that will need to be executed to accomplish the desired improvements. This gets filled into Step 6 of the 9-Step A3 (Figure 13.3).

Steps 7 and 8 focus on the execution of the improvement gaps that were identified in Steps 1–6. Step 7 manages the execution of the gaps identified in Step 6. It is the time and resource planning and the progress reporting for each of the improvements, including the assigning of these tasks to specific individuals who will be responsible for each task's completion.

At this point we should be ready to answer the following basic but critical questions about our gaps:

1. Do we have the resources to accomplish this task? If not, we need to escalate the shortage to our champion, and it is her problem to resolve the need.
2. What are the root causes behind this problem? We fix the root cause, not the symptoms.
3. Who needs to be involved in the solution (champions, facilitators, team members)? Do we need someone

outside the RIE team to make this change happen?
How do we get them involved?
4. What are the anticipated benefits of fixing this problem?
5. What tools or methodologies should be utilized?
6. What is the schedule or time line for execution? When
   will we accomplish our target improvements (Step 4)?

Step 8 links to Step 4. In Step 8 we are reporting on the metrics identified in Step 4 and demonstrating that improvements are actually being made. A fixed schedule, preferably monthly, should be set up for reviewing the progress for implementation. During this meeting the items in Step 7 of the A3 should be reviewed to see what is on schedule, what is off schedule, and what needs to have a revision to the schedule. These updates should be made, and completed tasks should be indicated. Step 8 should be updated with a progress report of the metrics that were listed in Step 4. This should be a "status at a glance" graphic, if possible, showing our target and indicating if we have reached our target.

Finally, Step 9 focuses on the postcompletion of the project. This is where we spread the knowledge that we gained by executing this improvement activity. We identify other areas in the organization that should also become the focus of a similar effort.

Executing the Rapid Improvement Event

At this point we have an extremely high-level view of the Lean process. A little more depth on how the RIE should be executed may be valuable. Here are some steps that should be followed:

An objective champion responsible for the execution of their corresponding tasks contacts a Lean facilitator, assigning them a task from the strategy map that requires a RIE improvement process to be executed.

The Lean facilitator starts filling out the first 4 steps of the A3, using it to perform the appropriate analysis of the selected task. As mentioned earlier in this chapter, this determines if a RIE will be required.

Assuming we will proceed with the RIE, the next step would be to develop a charter for the RIE process. This process is critical to the success of the RIE. The charter defines the expected results of the RIE. It defines ownership and requires champion sign-off. It defines the team involved and the expected timeline. It defines the metrics that will be used to define the success or failure of the improvement. The charter defines the makeup of the team and identifies the resources that will be required for the execution of the RIE. The charter is the sign-off where the champion agrees to the allocation of the necessary and required resources.

Running the RIE event normally includes the following:

1. Team introductions.
2. Training on Lean and the RIE process.
3. Defining and highlighting the expectations from the event.
4. Detailing out a SIPOC (suppliers, inputs, processes, outputs, customers). This is where the team thinks through who is the customer of this process, what are the outputs of this process, what are the required inputs of this process, and who are the suppliers of the inputs. This discussion helps the team to solidify the scope of the task being analyzed. The process is analyzed using the current-state value stream map (next step).
5. Current-state VSM (value stream map). What is the current process?
6. Future-state VSM. What is the desired future process?
7. Updating the 9-Step A3 with corrections in the first 4 boxes, filling in Steps 5 and 6, and starting the planning process of Step 7.
8. Monitor the improvement process to make sure the anticipated benefits are achieved (Steps 7 and 8).
9. Report the results of the RIE to the appropriate champions at the end of the event in the event room (referred to as the *Wall Walk* or *Walk the Wall*).

10. A fixed schedule, preferably monthly, should be set up for governance (ongoing review) of the progress for changes being implemented. Updates should be made and completed tasks should be indicated.
11. Step 8 of the A3 should be updated with a progress report of the metrics that were listed in Step 4. This should be a "status at a glance" graphic if possible showing our target and indicating whether we have reached our target.

Moving the Needle

By no means does this chapter do justice to the concept of Lean and the various tools that are part of the Lean toolkit. A clear understanding of all the elements of Lean requires a book of its own, and some were recommended in this chapter. The intent was to offer an overview of the power of Lean and how Lean should be the driver that executes the tasks of the strategy map. Hopefully the reader now has a clearer understanding of how execution will occur. And if your organization has Lean facilitators, it's time to put them to work. Other options include training one or more Lean facilitators or hiring a Lean organization to do the facilitation for you, which has the advantage of not bringing corporate and internal prejudices into the processes. But don't try to do a Lean event without an experienced facilitator. You will most likely be wasting a lot of valuable time and money, and you won't get the maximum benefit out of your effort.

In the end, the goal of the strategy map and the corresponding RIE and Lean efforts is to "move the needle." What this means is that we are trying to improve on the metrics listed in the strategy map (column 3) and ultimately achieve the goal of the priority (column 1 in the strategy map). And this book has given you the structure for accomplishing both of these.

Summary

This chapter has focused on making improvements. This is where we see a difference in the organization, where we see the metrics improve, where we see the goals achieved. The tool that the authors recommended for this improvement process is Lean. However, as mentioned, it is impossible in one chapter to describe perfectly how Lean should work. So this chapter focused on some Lean basics and on how this should be linked to the strategy map.

14
Repeating the
Strategic Cycle

Driving
Strategy
to Execution

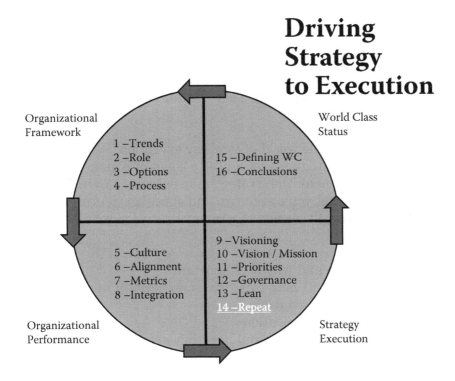

Organizational
Framework

World Class
Status

1 –Trends
2 –Role
3 –Options
4 –Process

15 –Defining WC
16 –Conclusions

5 –Culture
6 –Alignment
7 –Metrics
8 –Integration

9 –Visioning
10 –Vision / Mission
11 –Priorities
12 –Governance
13 –Lean
14 –Repeat

Organizational
Performance

Strategy
Execution

At this point we have successfully progressed through the development of a strategic plan and discussed the execution of the plan. What we have learned includes the following:

- How visioning works and what it is used for
- The purpose of scenario planning
- What a strategy map is and how it is used
- The importance and role of core competencies
- The composition of a vision
- The creation of a mission and the purpose it serves
- The importance of identifying who your customers are
- How to dissect your mission statement into three or four priorities
- The purpose and use of an end state statement
- The purpose and role of a priority-specific goal
- How to decompose a priority into three or four objective statements
- The purpose of an objective definition statement
- The use of metrics and how they are tied to the objective and to the priority's goal statement
- The role and importance of tasks and how they tie to a metrics statement

Next we entered the world of strategy execution. Without this component a strategy is just a pretty sheet of paper. With the execution component, the strategy map becomes a living, working document that you use to run and optimize your organization. During the discussion of strategy execution we discussed the following:

- Governance and why it's important
- Cascading and how this drives ownership at all levels of the organization
- Strategy communication
- Performance reviews and how they are executed
- The critical role of objective champions who own the efforts focused on improving a specific objective
- The execution of strategy map tasks through the use of Lean
- How the Lean process works

Front-End Strategic Information			
Core Competencies:			
Vision:			
Mission:			
Defining the Customer:			
The Strategy Map			
Priorities and Goals:	Objectives / Strategies:	Metrics:	Tasks / Action Items:
Priority Statement: End State Statement:	Objective / Strategy Statement:	Metrics Statements:	Tasks / Action Item Statements:
Goal Statement:	Objective / Strategy Statement:	Metrics Statements:	Tasks / Action Item Statements:
	Objective / Strategy Statement:	Metrics Statements:	Tasks / Action Item Statements:

Figure 14.1 The strategy map.

- How to monitor and control the Lean process by using the A3 or 9-Step Opportunity/Problem Analysis Tool (Figure 14.2)
- The role of a Lean facilitator
- The monitoring of the progress of the Lean event
- The linkage between the Lean event and the strategy map

But we are not finished. The strategy map (Figure 14.1) is a living document that requires regular updating. It is never completed. All the priorities are never met. All the goals are never achieved. Your organization is not yet ready to be escalated to organizational nirvana. There will always be things to change or improve. There will always be external factors that play on your markets. Best practices are constantly changing, and this constant level of change means that your top priorities today will not be your top priorities a year from now.

The solution is obvious. We need to see ourselves as an organic, constantly changing environment. As we can see in Figure 14.3, strategic planning is a continuous improvement process; it is a continuous cycle of changing and being

Team Members: Who are the individuals who worked on this 9-step report?	9-Step Opportunity (Problem) Analysis Tool	Approval Information/Signatures Who are the champions for (signers of) this Project?
1. Clarify & Validate the Problem State the basic overall fundamental problem that needs to be solved and validate that it is strategically aligned with the enterprise objectives.	5. Determine Root Cause Define the root-causes of the current problem and the reason for current performance gaps. What caused the need for this change?	7. Execute Improvement Tasks Prioritize the actions listed in step 6, time sequence them, identify specific completion dates, assign responsibility for the completion, and state where help is needed in order to complete the action. What are the deliverables and their due dates?
2. Perform a Purpose Expansion on the Problem Confirm that we are doing the right things.		
3. Break Down the Problem/Identify Performance Gaps What are the facts? List what specifically needs to change to solve the problem and what are the performance gaps to be closed to realize required performance. Prove it!	6. Develop Improvement Task List List the specific actions that need to be implemented to create change and close performance gaps. Validate that all the root causes listed in step 5 have been accounted for and resolved. What needs to change in order to eliminate the root cause?	8. Confirm Results Report progress made on the improvement targets listed in step 4. Confirm that we are doing the right things in the right way by improving the desired performance areas. Did you achieve your desired results? (At-a-glance status)
4. Set Improvement Targets Set improvement targets. Identify annual and long term stretch targets as appropriate.		9. Standardize Successful Processes List ways to institutionalize best practices and processes learned from implementing this change. How can we institutionalize this "best practice?"

Figure 14.2 Nine-Step A3 with definitions.

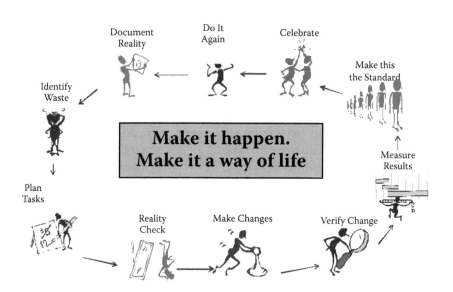

Figure 14.3 Strategic planning—a continuous improvement process.

changed. And we can either manage the change or have the change manage us. We can either be in control of our future or spend our time fighting fires. And fighting these fires is a nonstrategic process and is often counterproductive.

Summary

Strategic planning is a continuous, never-ending process. But that does not mean that you are caught in a doomsday spiral. Rather, it means that you now have the tools to grow your organization in a directed and focused manner. Now is the time to drive your organization to world class status.

PART IV

World Class
Strategy Status

15

Defining and Establishing World Class Status

Driving Strategy to Execution

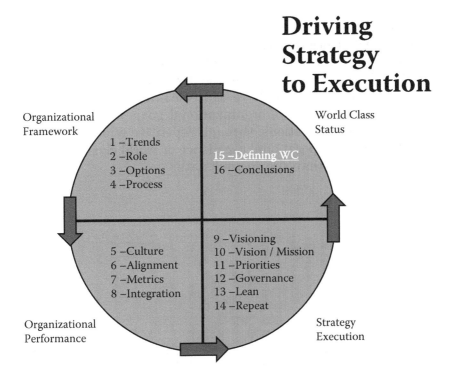

Organizational Framework

World Class Status

1 –Trends
2 –Role
3 –Options
4 –Process

15 –Defining WC
16 –Conclusions

5 –Culture
6 –Alignment
7 –Metrics
8 –Integration

9 –Visioning
10 –Vision / Mission
11 –Priorities
12 –Governance
13 –Lean
14 –Repeat

Organizational Performance

Strategy Execution

World class organizations are those that achieve high performance through operational excellence. They have organizational cultures that solve problems and continuously improve. They develop and execute strategies that overcome the barriers they face and achieve their operational and strategic objectives by aligning all elements of the organization toward common goals and objectives. Ultimately, they continue to lead by competing with themselves and continually challenging the boundaries of success.

In Chapter 6 we introduced the transformation curve. This curve, seen in Figure 15.1, shows the phases of transformation of an organization that is a stagnant status quo organization to one that has the attributes of world class described above.

We also described how organizations transition through the various phases of learning and development, from being status quo organizations that operate under the assumption that all is well, to being reactive organizations that begin to understand the tools of problem solving and continuous improvement and are able to apply them when conditions warrant. Proactive organizations are those that begin to embrace strategic planning and proactively prepare for and address pending issues. These are the organizations that are able to align their resources and drive strategic initiatives that enable them to set and achieve organizational goals and objectives. Progressive organizations, through repetitive efforts, achieve a state in which operational excellence or world class becomes the norm rather than the desired state.

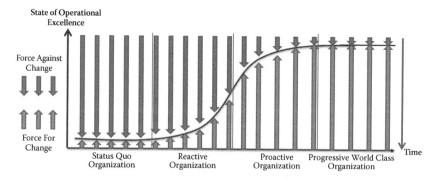

Figure 15.1 World class transformation.

As organizations begin to accept this model of transformation, the question "How do we know where we are on the curve?" always comes up. To answer that question, we had to delve into what the attributes are that define a culture of problem solving, continuous improvement, and effective leadership. The result of our efforts is the Model for Success (MFS) assessment tool, developed by members of the MainStream GS team, led by Dave Ringel.

The MFS assessment tool (Figure 15.2) is built on defining the value stream of creating high performance organizations and somewhat follows a DMAIC approach (define, measure, analyze, improve, and control). The series of steps in the process is as follows:

1. Generate a burning platform
2. Lead change from the top
3. Understand the current state
4. Set goals and make plans
5. Deploy the plans
6. Practice broad-based problem solving and waste reduction
7. Implement and follow through
8. Reach sustainment and validate results
9. Anchor the new methods

Under each of these steps is a series of attributes or actions based on the culture of problem solving and continuous improvement (Figure 15.3) that we defined in Chapter 8.

- Urgency
- Learning
- Discipline
- Empowerment
- Communication

As an example of how the model works under Step 1, generate a burning platform, the attributes are as follows:

- Urgency: Adopt the local case for change
- Learning: Leverage outside transformation experts

Model For Success - Creating High Performance Organizations MainStream

CONDUCTING CONTINUOUS IMPROVEMENT	0%	0%	0%	0%	0%	0%	0%	0%	0%	0%
URGENCY Leadership fosters a sense of URGENY	0	0	0	0	0	0	0	0	0	0%
LEARNING Acquire the necessary SUBJECT MATTER EXPERTISE	0	0	0	0	0	0	0	0	0	0%
DISCIPLINE Generate REPEATABILITY through diligence and standard work	0	0	0	0	0	0	0	0	0	0%
EMPOWERMENT Generate the WILL to succeed by embracing the value add levels	0	0	0	0	0	0	0	0	0	0%
COMMUNICATION Generate UNDERSTANDING through a continual flow of information	0	0	0	0	0	0	0	0	0	0%

Value = 5	5
Value = 4	4
Value = 3	3
Value = 2	2
Value = 1	1
Value = 0	0

Value > 80% - 100%	81%
Value > 60% - 80%	61%
Value > 40% - 60%	41%
Value > 20% - 40%	21%
Value > 0% - 20%	1%
Value = 0%	0%

Figure 15.2 Model for success: creating high-performance organizations.

Figure 15.3 Culture of problem solving and continuous improvement.

- Discipline: Develop and deploy communications standard work
- Empowerment: Establish a system for bottom-up communication
- Communication: Establish a system for top-down communication

Under each of these attributes there are a series of yes or no questions that when answered provide a 1–5 score for the organization. Based on the accumulated score for the entire assessment, the organization can see where it stands on the transformation curve, but can also identify areas of opportunity or focus for improving its position on the curve. To reflect specific differences in client organizations, the questions are tailored to the organization in which the assessment is being conducted.

From additional lessons learned we do not use this as a self-assessment tool because the value of the tool is in the independent look of an outsider looking in and responding to the questions with the eye of an expert.

The remaining steps and attribute markers from the table are as follows:

2. Lead change from the top
   - Establish governance teams
   - Establish a continuous process improvement (CPI) facilitation element
   - Develop and deploy change management standard work
   - Establish ground rules for deploying change
   - Publish the change management elements and emerging communications
3. Understand the current state
   - Conduct technical analysis and identify key performance indicators (KPIs)
   - Teach senior leaders
   - Agree on baselines and establish the flow of data
   - Conduct a cultural analysis
   - Publicize the baseline measurements
4. Set goals and make plans
   - Set the vision, mission, and improvement goals
   - Teach middle managers
   - Develop strategies to pursue the goals
   - Develop and deploy action plans to pursue the strategies
   - Publicize the strategy map and action plans
5. Deploy the plans
   - Lead with a bias for action
   - Teach team leads and champions
   - Develop and deploy change plans
   - Conduct targeted improvements
   - Publicize status of targeted improvements
6. Practice broad-based problem solving and waste reduction
   - Go regularly to the workplace (Gemba)
   - Teach Lean and problem solving to everybody
   - Develop and deploy leader standard work
   - Employ workplace Lean/Six Sigma tools
   - Employ Lean shop floor communications tools
7. Implement and follow through
   - Uphold accountability for results
   - Teach implementation and follow through
   - Develop and deploy implementation plans

- Monitor implementations
- Publicize implementation status
8. Reach sustainment and validate results
   - Uphold accountability for sustainment
   - Teach results validation
   - Quantify the impact of sustained results
   - Monitor sustainment
   - Report sustained results
9. Anchor the new methods
   - Sponsor benchmarking and integration
   - Teach benchmarking and integration
   - Update policy and standard work
   - Employ a recognition and rewards program
   - Update baselines

High scores on each of the elements of the assessment indicate that the organization has created a culture with continuous improvement capability with the urgency, skill, repeatability, will, and understanding required to drive and sustain improvement.

MainStream GS used this model to assess the progress of the various Wing organizations within the U.S. Air Force's Air Mobility Command over the course of their 5 year strategic transformation engagement with that command. From the assessments they were able to provide information to the command leadership as to where on the continuous improvement continuum each of their wing commanders and their respective organizations were. This helped the Air Mobility Command commander determine where he would apply additional consulting help and strategically determine what actions he needed to take to move the organization forward as a whole. Because limited resources were available, the decision the commander made was to focus support on key wings that were well on their way to executing their strategic plans. In doing so he was able to move the overall strategy alignment and deployment effort forward and use peer pressure to get the remaining wing commanders on board.

The assessment tool provided the measure of success but also provided the information needed to focus the available resources in the most efficient and effective manner to better execute the organization's strategic plans, overcome its barriers to success, and achieve its long-range objectives.

It is this world class culture that is capable of developing high performance through operational excellence, leveraging its Lean and Six Sigma capabilities to drive strategy execution.

16
Summary and Conclusion

Driving Strategy to Execution

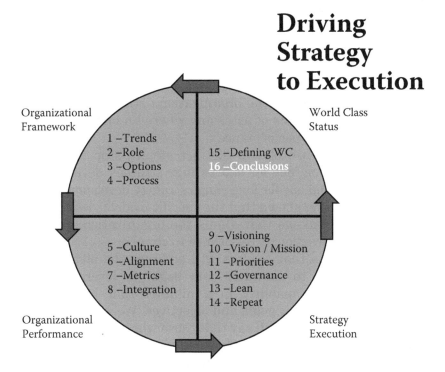

Organizational Framework

World Class Status

1 –Trends
2 –Role
3 –Options
4 –Process

15 –Defining WC
16 –Conclusions

9 –Visioning
10 –Vision / Mission
11 –Priorities
12 –Governance
13 –Lean
14 –Repeat

5 –Culture
6 –Alignment
7 –Metrics
8 –Integration

Organizational Performance

Strategy Execution

In this book we have provided a framework for driving strategy to execution. We have defined an organizational framework, organizational performance, strategy execution, and world class status as a framework for driving strategy to execution. We have explained why organizations leverage their

Lean and Six Sigma capability to drive strategy execution. We have shown how Lean eliminates waste and process variation more successfully than other execution strategies. We have identified the critical linkage between strategic planning and daily execution. We have shown that to successfully execute a strategic plan, an organization must have a consistent methodology, a strong governance system with the right metrics, and a means of overcoming the inherent resistance to change that exists in all organizations. We have also linked successful strategy execution to organizational alignment. Strategies should align to the value stream of an organization's products or services and demonstrate how well it is able to both effectively and efficiently utilize its available resources. Strategy linkage focuses on the daily execution of both the operational requirements of servicing its customers along with execution of its strategic plans and initiatives. We have demonstrated how critical it is to establish a culture of problem solving and continuous process improvement so that an organization has disciplined people following the disciplined processes required to execute and sustain the organization's strategies. And we have provided a means of assessing where an organization is on its path to high performance.

Through the use of two distinct step-by-step models of strategy execution, one for short-range strategy development and execution and one for long-range strategy development and execution, we have shown that the specific model is less important than the linkage that aligns the organization, governs execution, and overcomes resistance to change.

It is our hope that readers will embrace the elements of driving strategy to execution and begin to leverage their Lean/Six Sigma capability in a manner that helps them achieve their strategic goals and objectives. We won't say that it is easy to do, but we will say that those who stick with it will find that with each iteration they will get better and better at successfully executing their strategies and becoming a high-performance organization.

The time to begin is now.

About the Authors

Gerhard Plenert

Dr. Gerhard Plenert has more than 25 years of professional experience in information technology quality and productivity consulting and in working on manufacturing planning and scheduling methods. He also has 13 years of academic experience. He has more than 150 published articles and he has published the following 10 books

International Management and Production: Survival Techniques for Corporate America

The Plant Operations Deskbook (an APICS series book)

World Class Manager

Making Innovation Happen: Concept Management through Integration

Finite Capacity Scheduling (an APICS/Oliver White Series Book; 2000)

EManager: Value Chain Management in an eCommerce World (2001)

International Operations Management (an MBA textbook; 2004)

Operations Management (a United Nations training manual for developing country factories; 2005)

Reinventing Lean: Introducing Lean Management into the Supply Chain (2007)

Lean Management Principles for Information Technology (2011)

Dr. Plenert has extensive industry experience:

Private sector
  • Kraft Foods, Smart and Final, Davis Lay, Ritz-Carlton, Hewlett-Packard, Seagate, Motorola, PPI, Clark Equipment, NCR Corporation, AT&T
  • Consulting companies: Wipro Technologies, Infosys, MainStream Management, AMS, IBM, SCI, SAS
  • Practice partner for supply chain management and Lean/Six Sigma for Wipro
  • Corporate "guru" on supply chain management for AMS and Infosys

Government sector
  • California: DCSS, DHS
  • Federal: DSS, U.S. Air Force, U.S. Air National Guard
  • International: United Nations
  • Texas: OAG
  • New York: City of New York warehousing system

Dr. Plenert has extensive academic experience:

  • PhD in mineral economics at the Colorado School of Mines (their operations and business management degree; under Gene Woolsey)
  • Eleven years as a full-time faculty member (BYU and CSUC)
  • Currently teaching SCM at the University of San Diego
  • Teaching operations, manufacturing, and supply chain management as far away as Malaysia and England

Dr. Plenert has—

  • Worked in senior management
  • Generated up to triple the office productivity with the same staffing
  • Worked as an industry consultant implementing SCM, ERP and eBusiness systems and designing a next-generation enterprise model

- Literally "written the book" on leading-edge supply chain management concepts like finite capacity scheduling (FCS), advanced planning and scheduling (APS), and world class management
- Taken a 14+ percent defect rate down to 2 percent
- Brought setup times from 20 minutes to as low as 6 minutes
- Reduced facility-wide inventories by 40 percent

Dr. Plenert's ideas and publications have been endorsed by people like Steven Covey and companies like Motorola, AT&T, Black & Decker, and FedEx.

Contact information for Gerhard Plenert is as follows:

E-mail: TIOWCM@AOL.COM
Phone: 916-233-9758

Tom Cluley

Tom Cluley has more than 35 years of experience in operational leadership and management consulting. He has written numerous papers on leadership and creating high-performance organizations, and now this is his first book. Tom is the chief operations partner of MainStream GS, LLC, responsible as the technical lead for consulting work performed by the company's team of senior management and Lean/Six Sigma consultants. Tom became an expert in Lean methodologies and Hoshin Kanri under the tutelage of Shingijutsu masters as a director of operations and materials within the Wiremold Company, and is a certified Lean/Six Sigma master black belt. He is an experienced senior management consultant, coaching and mentoring all levels of client organizations through successful transformations to high performance. Tom has extensive experience guiding both commercial and public-sector executive leadership in strategy alignment and deployment as a means to align organizational efforts and successfully

leverage continuous process improvement (CPI) methodologies to accomplish organizational objectives. He is an expert
at integrating CPI methodologies (Lean, Six Sigma, TOC, and
others) with the development of robust governance systems
while applying organizational change management tools and
methods to help overcome barriers to success and create cultural acceptance.

Contact information for Tom Cluley is as follows:

Chief Operations Partner, MainStream GS, LLC
Phone: 856-296-1144
Fax: 480-924-2468
E-mail: tomcluley@aol.com

Index